Baylor Scott & White Health has again provided a road map, this time exceptionally documented and annotated. This effort will assist health care institutions in consistently improving the care provided to their patients. In today's ultra-competitive world focused on the right care at the right time in the right setting, Baylor Scott & White Health's second effort is a must read. It provides both the rational and in-depth tools to transform an organization into a world-class provider of safe and efficient health care services. Combined with strong patient and family participation, it offers the road map to substantially improved patient satisfaction, staff retention and community endorsement. Kudos to Dr. Ballard and his team—a clear, clean, and crisp presentation.

Arja P. Adair, Jr., MBA
President and Founder
TOKOBE, LLC
Retired President/CEO
CFMC

Achieving best clinical outcomes at lower costs, while creating an ideal patient and provider experience, requires a set of intentional structures and processes. Dr. Ballard and his team have developed the "How-To Manual."

Ziad Haydar, MD, MBA
Senior Vice President and Chief Medical Officer
Ascension Health

This guide to achieving STEEEP health care lays out a very practical approach to patient safety and quality improvement based on the extensive experience of Dr. Ballard and his team. The practical examples included in this guide are a gold mine of useful approaches for any health care system wondering where to start or how to take the next step in their journey. This companion to the earlier book should be welcomed by many waking up to the importance of driving change in the delivery of care at the present time.

J. Michael Henderson, MD
Chief Quality Officer
Cleveland Clinic

Organizations that can reliably and effectively implement best practices will be leaders in the health care field in the 21st century. This book is a gold mine of practical and valuable resources and tools for health care organizations to use today and for years to come in their improvement journeys.

Maulik Joshi, DrPH
President
Health Research and Educational Trust
Senior Vice President of Research
American Hospital Association

For quality leaders who are wondering what to do and how to do it—this book provides the detail that you have been seeking, right down to the level of the types of people to hire, what their qualifications should be, where they should fit in the governance chart, and the nature of their deliverables.

Thomas H. Lee, MD
Chief Medical Officer
Press Ganey Associates, Inc.

Baylor Scott & White Health's journey to improve health care guided by the Institute of Medicine's STEEEP aims serves as a role model for all of us in health care. But then comes the hard part—implementation. The practical, well-organized suggestions contained in this guide, harvested from the organization's real-life experience, are an invaluable resource for others considering a similar journey. The guide is helpful for anyone, novice or expert, who is helping to lead large-scale clinical change in today's challenging health care environment.

Gary Yates, MD
President
Sentara Quality Care Network
President
Healthcare Performance Improvement, LLC
Former Senior Vice President and Chief Medical Officer
Sentara Healthcare

The Guide to Achieving **STEEP** Health Care

Baylor Scott & White Health's Quality Improvement Journey

David J. Ballard, MD, PhD

CRC Press
Taylor & Francis Group
Boca Raton London New York

CRC Press is an imprint of the
Taylor & Francis Group, an **informa** business

A PRODUCTIVITY PRESS BOOK

CRC Press
Taylor & Francis Group
6000 Broken Sound Parkway NW, Suite 300
Boca Raton, FL 33487-2742

CRC Press is an imprint of Taylor & Francis Group, an Informa business

No claim to original U.S. Government works

Printed on acid-free paper
Version Date: 20141015

International Standard Book Number-13: 978-1-4822-3681-1 (Paperback)

This book contains information obtained from authentic and highly regarded sources. Reasonable efforts have been made to publish reliable data and information, but the author and publisher cannot assume responsibility for the validity of all materials or the consequences of their use. The authors and publishers have attempted to trace the copyright holders of all material reproduced in this publication and apologize to copyright holders if permission to publish in this form has not been obtained. If any copyright material has not been acknowledged please write and let us know so we may rectify in any future reprint.

Library of Congress Cataloging-in-Publication Data

Ballard, David J., author.
    The guide to achieving STEEEP health care : Baylor Scott & White Health's quality Improvement journey / author, David J. Ballard.
       p. ; cm.
    Companion book to: Achieving STEEEP health care / David J. Ballard, editor ; associate editors, Neil S. Fleming, Joel T. Allison, Paul B. Convery, Rosemary Luquire. 2014.
    Includes bibliographical references and index.
    ISBN 978-1-4822-3681-1 (alk. paper)
    I. Achieving STEEEP health care. Complemented by (work): II. Title.
    [DNLM: 1. Baylor Scott & White Health. 2. Hospital Administration--methods. 3. Quality of Health Care. 4. Hospitals--standards. 5. Patient-Centered Care. WX 153]

RA971
362.11068--dc23

2014024627

Visit the Taylor & Francis Web site at
http://www.taylorandfrancis.com

and the CRC Press Web site at
http://www.crcpress.com

Contents

This book is a practical guide for delivering health care that is safe, timely, effective, efficient, equitable, and patient centered (STEEEP).

Baylor Scott & White Health (BSWH), founded when Baylor Health Care System (BHCS) and Scott & White Healthcare joined in 2013, has more than 100 years of experience progressing through its own STEEEP Quality Journey and developing strategies, methods, and tools for operationalizing the delivery of STEEEP care. Along with its commitment to STEEEP care, the organization is guided by its vision to be the most trusted name in giving and receiving safe, quality, compassionate health care and its mission to serve all people by providing personalized health and wellness through exemplary care, education, and research as a Christian ministry of healing.

As part of its long-standing commitment to health care quality, BHCS hired David J. Ballard, MD, MSPH, PhD, FACP, in 2000 as its first chief quality officer. Dr. Ballard chaired the ad hoc committee established by the BHCS Board of Trustees to develop a strategic plan that would advance the organization's goal "to deliver the best and safest care available, focusing on wellness, prevention, early detection, acute and subacute care, and supported at every point by education, research, and improvement." The strategic plan recommended the alignment of board, administrative, and clinician leaders toward making care quality a top organizational priority; a redesign of the executive compensation program to align with health care improvement objectives; and the creation of an organization-wide committee to monitor and improve the quality of patient care by designing, developing, and implementing quality improvement initiatives throughout BHCS.

To realize the goals of the strategic plan and ensure the delivery of ideal care as defined by national evidence-based standards, BHCS embraced the Institute of Medicine's aims of health care that is safe, timely, effective, efficient, equitable, and patient centered. Envisioning the analogy of climbing a steep mountain, BHCS leaders created the STEEEP acronym in 2000 and have used this framework to guide the organization's quality improvement journey ever since.

The success of health care quality improvement initiatives developed to make care more STEEEP has led BHCS to receive several regional and national awards, including the 2008 National Quality Forum National Quality Healthcare Award, which recognizes exemplary health care organizations that are role models for achieving meaningful and sustainable quality improvement in health care, and the inaugural Leapfrog Patient-Centered Care Award, given to a health system whose board has most successfully driven the creation of a true partnership between patients and their caregivers. During Dr. Ballard's tenure as chief quality officer, BHCS and its affiliated physician group HealthTexas Provider Network was also named as a 2014 American Medical Group Association Acclaim Award Honoree and won the 2010 Preeminence Award of the American Medical Group Association, awarded to physician–administrator leadership teams for exceptional leadership, innovation and vision, contributions to the advancement of quality, effective health care delivery practices and structure, and outstanding contributions to the local community.

To advance its mission to serve all people by providing personalized health and wellness through exemplary care, education, and research, BHCS founded the STEEEP Global Institute in 2012. Today, the STEEEP Global Institute leverages the expertise and experience of BSWH to assist other organizations in improving health care quality. It collaborates with domestic and international partners to identify and solve problems in health care delivery with the ultimate goal of making health care more STEEEP. Additional information and resources related to STEEEP care can be found at http://www.STEEEPGlobalInstitute.com.

Acknowledgments

This guide book was made possible by the efforts of more than 36,000 employees across Baylor Scott & White Health (BSWH) who are committed to the organization's vision to be the most trusted name in giving and receiving safe, quality, compassionate health care. I am grateful to them as well as to the BSWH leaders who embraced the tenets of STEEEP (safe, timely, effective, efficient, equitable, patient-centered) care in 2000 and who have guided the organization's quality journey according to those principles ever since.

I am appreciative of the efforts of the individual employees who provided examples of their daily contributions to the BSWH STEEEP quality journey in the form of presentations, case studies, and tools for improving STEEEP care. In addition, I am grateful to Nanette Myers, Jack Rahaim, Kathleen Richter, and Alyssa Zarro, who provided editorial support during the production of this book.

Introduction

STEEEP® QUALITY JOURNEY

This book is a road map for delivering health care that is safe, timely, effective, efficient, equitable, and patient centered (STEEEP). According to the Institute of Medicine (IOM) (Corrigan et al. 2001), STEEEP care is care that is

- **Safe**—avoiding injury to patients from care that is intended to help them, without accidental error or inadvertent exposures
- **Timely**—reducing waits and harmful delays that have an impact on smooth flow of care
- **Effective**—providing services based on scientific knowledge to all who could benefit and refraining from providing services to those not likely to benefit (avoiding overuse and underuse)
- **Efficient**—using resources to achieve best value by reducing waste and reducing production and administrative costs
- **Equitable**—providing care that does not vary in quality according to personal characteristics such as gender, income, ethnicity, or location
- **Patient Centered**—providing care that is respectful of and responsive to individual patient preferences, needs, and values

This guide serves as a companion to the book *Achieving STEEEP Health Care*, published by CRC Press in September 2013, which describes the Baylor Scott & White Health (BSWH) journey to delivering STEEEP care (Ballard et al. 2013). To complement that book, this guide provides a template for creating a quality improvement (QI) program scalable to the size and scope of any health care organization. It describes:

- The roles of administrative, board, clinician, and quality leaders in driving and sustaining organization-wide QI
- The programs and expertise needed to support a comprehensive QI program
- The data and analytics required to measure QI and to develop and refine a QI program
- The role of reputation and accreditation in validating the program's outcomes

Non-US-Based and Non-Hospital-Based Organizations

Many copies of this guide's companion book *Achieving STEEEP Health Care* have been purchased by readers outside the United States. The strategies and tools presented in this guide, with some allowance for cultural and legal differences (e.g., in the area of data capture), are applicable to non-US-based organizations. The imperative to deliver high-quality care at a low cost exists throughout the world. Although the dynamics driving health care QI in the United States involve unique competitive circumstances and legislative initiatives (e.g., the Affordable Care Act), the need for high-quality health care driven by patient, family, and community involvement is universal.

In addition, although this guide was developed based on lessons learned from a health care delivery system, other health care organizations (e.g., accountable care organizations [ACOs], medical groups, skilled nursing facilities) can enhance quality throughout their institutions by applying its recommendations. In today's constantly evolving health care environment, any organization that is part of the continuum of care has a need to improve quality consistent with STEEEP aims. In addition to benefiting patients, a commitment to continuous QI is likely to be required by partner organizations, regulatory agencies, and policy initiatives.

HOW TO USE THIS GUIDE

This guide has been structured to allow you to access information based on your specific needs. This allows for a number of approaches:

- You can read the guide in its entirety to learn about the STEEEP Quality Journey.
- You can focus on a specific phase to analyze the successful components required to advance to the next phase of the STEEEP Quality Journey (Table I.1).
- You can focus on your role to learn what you can do to drive the QI effort from your position in the organization (Table I.2).

Baylor Scott & White Health

The lessons BSWH has learned during its STEEEP Quality Journey are relevant to any organization pursuing the delivery of high-quality health care, regardless of size or geographic location. In particular, the need to regard QI as a journey applicable to the entire health care delivery system rather than simply a collection of tools, methods, and techniques is a core theme of this guide.

BSWH began its journey to STEEEP care over a century ago with the founding of its constituent organizations, Baylor Health Care System (BHCS) and Scott & White Healthcare (SWH). BHCS has been dedicated to providing high-quality health care to the residents of Dallas–Fort Worth, Texas, since it opened its doors in 1903. The organization reached an important milestone in its quality journey in 2000, when it created and trademarked the acronym STEEEP to communicate the challenge of delivering ideal health care in terms of the analogy of climbing a steep mountain, aligned with the IOM's six aims for a high-performing twenty-first-century health care system (Corrigan et al. 2001). Like BHCS, SWH has a long-standing history of dedication to patient care and continuous improvement in quality and patient safety. Founded in 1897, SWH provides central Texans with personalized, comprehensive, high-quality care enhanced by medical education and research.

In 2013, BHCS and SWH joined to create a system able to meet the demands of health care reform, the changing needs of patients, and extraordinary recent advances in clinical care. BSWH is now the largest not-for-profit health care system in Texas and one of the largest in the United States. It includes 43 hospitals, more than 500 patient care sites, 6,000 affiliated physicians, 36,000 employees, and the Scott & White Health Plan. This plan provides coverage to over 200,000 Texans. BSWH is guided by its vision to be the most trusted name in

TABLE I.1 The STEEEP Quality Journey

	Phase 1 Initiation	Phase 2: Foundation Building	Phase 3: Operationalizing	Phase 4: Continuous Quality Improvement
Administration and Governance	• Often unaware of potential benefits of quality improvement (QI) • Often do not view QI as their responsibility and instead delegate to clinicians	• Understand the necessity of becoming involved in and providing leadership in QI • Become engaged in QI initiatives	• Directly involved in driving the organization to a culture of QI • Actively measure and reward improvement	• Fully engaged in, and see themselves as accountable for driving, QI • Quality is an integral part of their and the organization's incentive program
Physician and Nurse Leadership	• Often have marginal involvement in QI initiatives • Focus is primarily on clinical delivery and organizational issues	• Active engagement in some QI initiatives • Represent the clinicians and the patient in QI discussions and decisions	• Work together to identify and lead QI initiatives • Become the voice of the patient as well as the clinician	• Fully engaged in QI and drive innovation within their disciplines • Often responsible for engaging their professional communities in QI efforts
Quality Improvement Programs and Expertise	• Limited QI knowledge • Few formally established QI measurement tools and methodologies • Limited or basic safety programs in place	• Pockets of QI expertise • Formal QI structure in place with limited measurable impact • Quality and safety programs across some disciplines or facilities • Some best practice initiatives	• Deeper expertise shared across disciplines or facilities • Formal structure in place with moderate QI • Organization-wide quality and safety programs	• Established governance and infrastructure for managing and coordinating QI • Formalized QI training for staff at multiple levels • Fully integrated processes, practices, data and analytics • Decision support drives innovation
Data and Analytics	• Little or no ability to extract relevant data and report on quality measures • Data integrity often an issue and a point of debate	• Outcomes/quality measurement and reporting in some areas • Infrastructure capable of extracting data, but with little or no analysis or potential for organizational impact	• Ability to extract and analyze data to drive QI initiatives • Data integrity no longer an issue and accepted in most areas of the organization	• Established procedures and timelines for data collection and analysis • Development and implementation of data-driven, clinical and operational best practices • Data are used to drive the incentive system for the organization
Reputation/Accreditation	• Basic/minimal accreditation	• Local reputation • Some advanced accreditation	• Regional reputation • Advanced accreditation in several areas	• Nationally recognized as a leader in quality, safety and innovation

TABLE I.2 Action Items for Organizational Leaders in Each Phase of the STEEEP Quality Journey

	Phase 1: Initiation	Phase 2: Foundation Building	Phase 3: Operationalizing	Phase 4: Continuous QI
• Administration and Governance	• Develop an awareness of the importance of QI to your organization • Participate in education programs focusing on QI's application to health care • Commit the organization to pursuing a path toward excellence in quality and patient safety that will culminate in Phase 4: Continuous QI • Create a board resolution that challenges the organization to achieve the highest levels of quality and patient safety • Set macro-level organizational quality and patient safety goals • Form a QI governance council • Develop an organizational QI entity	• Continue to learn about QI by participating in education programs and seeking advanced leadership training • Set moderately aggressive quality, patient safety, and patient experience goals • Continue to develop a culture of QI by linking financial incentives to quality, patient safety, and patient experience • Establish a formal governance structure for quality and patient safety • Include patient and families in QI efforts • Drive toward measurement and reporting that will highlight successes and opportunities	• Provide funding and support to achieve Phase 3 quality, patient safety, and patient experience goals and launch the organization to Phase 4 • Inculcate and embed a culture of quality, patient safety, and patient centeredness throughout the organization • Evaluate and refine QI metrics and commit to a quantitative approach to goal setting • Insist on transparency of quality, patient safety, and patient experience data to enable internal comparisons and drive organization-wide QI • Engage patients in discussions and decisions about the QI program	• Sustain an organizational culture that embraces and advances quality, patient safety, and patient experience at all levels • Spread QI successes by acknowledging achievements and the people responsible for them • Promote accountability for QI by hardwiring variable pay and a quantitative approach to organizational goal setting • Continuously drive a care partnership with patients and families • Measure and publicize the link between quality and cost

Physician and Nurse Leadership			
• Develop an awareness of the importance of QI to your organization • Participate in education programs focusing on QI • Hire/develop high-level clinician leaders • Assess and define your role in organizational QI • Take a leadership role in gaining commitment from your board and administrative leaders for the QI program • Put in place a structure to provide leadership to other clinicians • Participate in QI council and programs with your nonclinician colleagues • Put in place a structure to provide leadership to other clinicians • Initiate QI projects within your network of colleagues	• Take a more public QI leadership role • Engage in formal clinician leadership training that includes education in finance • Collaborate with administrative and quality leaders to set annual quality, patient safety, and patient experience goals for the organization • Establish teams of individuals from throughout the organization focused on QI and encourage active participation • Evolve your QI focus from point solutions to solutions that are more systemic and that have an impact on a larger portion of the continuum of care	• Drive a model of shared governance throughout the organization • Leverage the effectiveness of your QI efforts by expanding your focus organization-wide • Expand your circle of influence across the organization through participation in committees and other multidisciplinary groups • Create and strengthen relationships with finance leaders and leaders of core business support functions • Serve as the "voice of the patient" in discussions and decisions about QI	• Continuously drive organizational goal setting with your clinical expertise, QI experience, and role as patient advocate • Drive innovation within your discipline, both inside and outside the organization • Continuously define, refine, and implement evidence-based best practices throughout the organization • Establish and lead service-line quality improvement councils to foster a stronger connection among the elements of STEEEP care

Continued

TABLE I.2 *(Continued)* Action Items for Organizational Leaders in Each Phase of the STEEEP Quality Journey

	Phase 1: Initiation	Phase 2: Foundation Building	Phase 3: Operationalizing	Phase 4: Continuous QI
• **Quality Improvement Programs and Expertise**	• Hire/develop a chief quality officer • Hire/develop a director of QI • Hire/develop a QI coordinator • Approve the macro-level goals set, prioritized and agreed to by the board and administration • Provide education programs to train administrative and clinician leaders in QI • Establish ability to perform data collection, abstraction, and reporting • Ensure the organization meets basic performance benchmarks for quality and patient safety	• Collaborate with administrative and quality leaders to set annual quality, patient safety, and patient experience goals for the organization • Hire/develop QI and patient safety staff • Ensure that QI education personnel have experience in achieving QI as well as in educating others • Open the door to patient and family involvement in the QI program • Deploy a patient safety culture survey • Deploy an adverse event measurement tool • Improve equitable care throughout the community	• Make education in QI mandatory for all senior-level administrative and clinician leaders and provide QI training for additional leaders • Provide senior-level administrative and clinician leaders with continuing education about QI • Dedicate infrastructure and resources to an organization-wide patient safety department • Dedicate infrastructure and resources to an organization-wide patient experience department	• Continuously refine the QI program to enable the organization to reach and exceed performance established by national benchmarks • Continuously develop infrastructure for coordinating the QI program • Provide formal QI training for staff at multiple levels • Spread successful QI initiatives by fostering and rewarding improvement • Utilize decision support tools to drive innovation and STEEEP care

Data and Analytics	• Develop department and systems to measure, analyze, and report organizational performance as well as the effects of specific QI initiatives • Develop capabilities critical to organizing, using, and reporting existing organizational quality data • Define and identify performance metrics • Identify requirements for data collection	• Develop infrastructure for data collection and analysis • Support administrative, clinician, and quality leaders in interpreting outcomes of QI initiatives • Provide measurement support for the patient safety culture survey • Support organizational assessment of adverse events, inpatient mortality, and patient experience	• Enhance ability to extract and analyze data to drive QI initiatives • Establish data governance policies and procedures • Employ reporting methods that make data interactive, dynamic and drillable • Develop facility and service-line performance reports for organizational leaders • Use comparative date to improve patient care	• Support the establishment and maintenance of data-driven clinical and operational best practices • Use data to promote a proactive organizational approach to health care QI that is policy driven • Develop resources and technology to utilize large data sets and integrate data from multiple sources • Develop advanced analytic capabilities that include financial modeling abilities
Reputation and Accreditation	• Establish your organization with accrediting agencies as one that priorities the delivery of STEEEP care	• Build local reputation through community affiliations, relationships with key stakeholders, and employee engagement • Identify and apply for advanced accreditation	• Build regional reputation through quality awards and recognition • Further develop focus on health quality • Achieve additional advanced accreditation and certification	• Apply for national quality awards and recognition • Tell the story of your organization's STEEEP Quality Journey

giving and receiving safe, quality, compassionate health care; its mission to serve all people by providing personalized health and wellness through exemplary care, education, and research as a Christian ministry of healing; and an unwavering commitment to STEEEP health care.

Road Map for STEEEP Health Care

This guide describes the road map BSWH has followed to operationalize the delivery of STEEEP care by identifying the four phases of the STEEEP Quality Journey (Initiation, Foundation Building, Operationalizing, and Continuous QI) (Table I.1); the leaders and stake-holders and their roles in the journey (Administration and Governance, Physician and Nurse Leadership, QI Programs and Expertise, Data and Analytics, and Reputation/Accreditation); and the actions and goals appropriate to each phase (Table I.2).

Non-US-Based and Non-Hospital-Based Organizations

Non-US-based organizations are encouraged to adjust STEEEP Quality Journey roles and components to align with their specific cultural or legal situations. Readers from smaller organizations or from ACOs or medical groups should remember that although the particular roles discussed in this guide may vary with scale or organizational mission, the need for administrative, clinician, and quality leadership with board direction and oversight is critical to any health care organization. This guide includes specific suggestions for how smaller organizations, ACOs, or medical groups might approach the different phases of the STEEEP Quality Journey.

Table I.1 can be used in both a descriptive and a prescriptive manner: It can be descriptive, helping you to locate your organization's place in the journey based on the characteristics of specific phases; or, it can serve as a prescriptive tool, providing the characteristics your organization will need to adopt to migrate from one phase to the next.

One key lesson BSWH has learned on its journey to STEEEP health care is that the five components of health care delivery (Administration and Governance, Physician and Nurse Leadership, QI Programs and Expertise, Data and Analytics, and Reputation and Accreditation) must evolve together to facilitate successful, sustainable QI. A successful QI program also depends on collaboration among administrative, clinician, and quality leaders, supported by a robust data and analytics infrastructure as well as ongoing organizational attention to reputation and accreditation. Table I.2 depicts a checklist of actions that stakeholders from each role can use to help drive their organizations through the four phases of the STEEEP Quality Journey (Initiation, Foundation Building, Operationalizing, and Continuous QI).

David Joseph Ballard, MD, MSPH, PhD, FACP, was appointed on October 1, 2013, as chief quality officer of Baylor Scott & White Health (BSWH), the largest not-for-profit health care system in Texas, which includes 43 hospitals, 500 patient care sites, 6,000 affiliated physicians, 36,000 employees, and the Scott & White health plan. A native of Lexington, Kentucky, David graduated with academic distinction from the Lawrenceville School, where he was selected as its outstanding junior (Harvard Prize) and senior (Brainard Prize) by the faculty and as its outstanding senior (Yale Aurelian Award) by his classmates. He was All-State in baseball and football and was chosen by the National Football Foundation's Delaware Valley Chapter as its outstanding secondary school scholar–athlete in 1974. A board-certified internist, he trained at the Mayo Graduate School of Medicine following completion of degrees in chemistry, economics, epidemiology, and medicine at the University of North Carolina (UNC), where he was a Morehead Scholar, North Carolina Fellow, and junior year Phi Beta Kappa inductee. David held progressive academic appointments as assistant and then associate professor at the Mayo Medical School, as associate professor with tenure at the University of Virginia School of Medicine, and as professor of medicine with tenure in the Emory University School of Medicine and professor of epidemiology in the Rollins School of Public Health of Emory University. He joined the Baylor Health Care System (BHCS) in 1999 as its first chief quality officer. He serves on the Board of Managers of the Heart Hospital Baylor Plano and of the BHCS–Kessler/Select rehabilitation and long-term care joint venture. David also is a member of the executive committee of the High Value Healthcare Collaborative.

BHCS has been recognized by many organizations for its health care improvement accomplishments under David's leadership, including the 2007 Leapfrog Patient-Centered Care Award, the 2008 National Quality Healthcare Award of the National Quality Forum, and the 2010 Medical Group Preeminence Award of the American Medical Group Association. In July 2011, David was appointed as president of the BHCS, now BSWH, STEEEP Global Institute, to provide health care performance improvement solutions to health care organizations throughout the world. In 2012, he was selected as chair of the newly formed BHCS STEEEP/Best Care Governance Council to set strategy and direction for operational functions related to STEEEP (safe, timely, effective, efficient, equitable, patient-centered) care across BHCS, which is now scaled across BSWH under David's leadership.

David serves on the editorial boards of *Health Services Research,* the *Journal of Comparative Effectiveness Research*, and the *Mayo Clinic Proceedings* (as Health Policy Section editor). He is a 1995 recipient of the AcademyHealth New Investigator Award, given annually to the outstanding health services research scholar in the United States less than 40 years of age and a 2012 recipient of the John M. Eisenberg Article-of-the-Year in *Health Services Research*. His book, *Achieving STEEEP Health Care*, which was published in 2013, achieved the Shingo Research Award for its contributions to operational excellence. David's leadership roles have included service as founding head of the Mayo Section of Health Services Evaluation and as senior associate consultant and then consultant in the Mayo Department of Health Science Research (1986–1991); founding president, Kerr L. White Institute for Health Services Research (1991–1999); president (2001–2003) of the International Society for Quality in Health Care; chair of the Agency for Healthcare Research and Quality's (AHRQ's) Health Care Quality and Effectiveness Research study section (2006–2010); and most recently, Review Panel chair for the Patient Centered Care Outcomes Research Institute and for AHRQ's RFA-HS-12-004 (Building the Science of Public Reporting). He is 2013–2014 chair of AHRQ's Centers for Education and Research on Therapeutics Steering Committee and a 2014–2017 member of AHRQ's National Advisory Council. He has been a member of many National Quality Forum (NQF) committees, including its National Quality Healthcare Award Blue Ribbon Review Panel and National Voluntary Consensus Standards for Hospital Care: Specialty Physician Measures, which he cochaired. He cochaired the Joint Commission's Blood Management Performance Measures Project Technical Advisory Panel. David has also served as a member of the American Hospital Association's Dick Davidson Quality Milestone Award for Allied Association Leadership selection committee for 2011 and 2012. He currently serves as expert panelist for the American Idol in Medicine project of the Stanford University Clinical Excellence Research Center funded by the Peter G. Peterson Foundation. He is a member of the UNC School of Public Health Foundation Board and past member of the Board of Trustees of the Lawrenceville School and of the Texas Hospital Association. In 2008, David received the Distinguished Alumnus Award of the UNC School of Medicine.

Chapter 1

Phase 1 of the STEEEP Quality Journey
The Initiation Phase

INTRODUCTION TO PHASE 1: INITIATION

None of the phases in the STEEEP (safe, timely, effective, efficient, equitable, and patient centered) Quality Journey is easy to navigate, but the Initiation Phase (Figure 1.1) entails a unique set of challenges that result from bringing an organization to greater levels of awareness and focus to achieve high-quality health care delivery and improved patient outcomes. Although health care organizations have become increasingly aware of the importance of high-quality care delivery and the penalties associated with the failure to achieve superior outcomes, few fully appreciate how recent changes in legislation, market dynamics, competition, and a focus on improved population health have accelerated the need to engage their organizations in a profound focus on continuous quality improvement (QI). Organizations in Phase 1 of the STEEEP Quality Journey are focused on several efforts simultaneously. They must plan and begin building the necessary pieces of a QI program with a focus on achieving success in this phase, which will depend largely on efforts to educate administrative, clinical, and quality leaders about the importance of a QI program to the health care organization; at the same time, they must prepare for migration to Phase 2 and beyond.

As an organization begins its journey, it needs to give careful thought to organizing and staffing for Phase 1 and to making choices that will support the progression to continuously improving patient care. The structure of the organization—starting with centralized governance—drives QI. Many health care delivery organizations have the will to drive certain QI initiatives but struggle because they lack the proper organizational structure. For this reason, many Phase 1 QI efforts will focus on developing this governance and administrative support structure. Other foundational elements of the Initiation Phase of the STEEEP Quality Journey include the following:

- Strong board member stewardship and participation in the QI program
- Administrative responsibility and accountability for the QI program
- Strong physician and nurse leader participation in the QI program
- Strong quality leadership and a focused QI resource
- Strong participation of individuals involved with finance (i.e., the chief financial officer) in the QI program
- Creation of a culture that values awareness, education, and communication regarding the role of QI in health care

You Are Here

	INITIATION	FOUNDATION BUILDING	OPERATIONALIZING	CONTINUOUS QI
Administration and Governance	• Often unaware of potential benefits of QI • Often do not view QI as their responsibility and instead delegate to clinicians	• Understand the necessity of becoming involved in and providing leadership in QI • Become engaged in QI initiatives	• Directly involved in driving the organization to a culture of QI • Actively measure and reward improvement	• Fully engaged in, and see themselves as accountable for driving QI • Quality is an integral part of their, and the organization's incentive program
Physician and Nurse Leadership	• Often have marginal involvement in QI initiatives • Focus is primarily on clinical delivery and organizational issues	• Active engagement in some QI initiatives • Represent the clinicians and the patient in QI discussions and decisions	• Work together to identify and lead QI initiatives • Become the voice of the patient as well as the clinician	• Fully engaged in QI and drive innovation within their disciplines • Often responsible for engaging their professional communities in QI efforts
Quality Improvement Programs and Expertise	• Limited QI knowledge • Few formally established QI measurement tools and methodologies • Limited or basic safety programs in place	• Pockets of QI expertise • Formal QI structure in place with limited measureable impact • Quality and safety programs across some disciplines and/or facilities • Some best practice initiatives	• Deeper expertise shared across disciplines and/or facilities • Formal structure in place with moderate QI • Organization-wide quality and safety programs	• Established governance and infrastructure for managing and coordinating QI • Formalized QI training for staff at multiple levels • Fully integrated processes, practices, data and analysis • Decision support drives innovation
Data and Analytics	• Little or no ability to extract relevant data and report on quality measures • Data integrity often an issue and a point of debate	• Outcomes/quality measurement and reporting in some areas • Infrastructure capable of extracting data, but with little or no analysis or potential for organizational impact • Quality of data improving and slowly becoming accepted in a number of areas of the organization	• Ability to extract and analyze data to drive QI initiatives • Data integrity no longer an issue and accepted in most areas of the organization	• Established procedures and timelines for data collection and analysis • Development and implementation of data-driven, clinical and operational best practices • Data is used to drive the incentive system for the organization
Reputation/Accreditation	• Basic/minimal accreditation	• Local reputation • Some advanced accreditation	• Regional reputation • Advanced accreditation in several areas	• Nationally recognized as a leader in quality, safety and innovation

FIGURE 1.1 Initiation Phase of the STEEEP Quality Journey.

- Establishment of a data and analytics infrastructure to support the measurement and reporting of performance data
- Focused attention on the role of accreditation in developing the QI program

Other Organizations

One of the hallmarks of today's health care environment is the need for integration across the continuum of care driven by trends such as population management and bundling of care. Such trends are driving organizations to achieve QI not only for its own benefits but also as a requirement for participation in clinical partnerships with other health care delivery institutions. Clinical integration with other institutions depends on quality in your organization's operations as well as the ability to assimilate clinical data across organizational boundaries. Most important, each of these organizations and institutions needs to be connected closely to patients, families, and communities.

THE INITIATION PHASE: THE ADMINISTRATION AND GOVERNANCE ROLE IN THE STEEEP QUALITY JOURNEY

Develop an Awareness of the Importance of QI to Your Organization

At the start of the Initiation Phase, administrative leaders and board members may not fully recognize the importance of QI to the organization and may not yet appreciate the significance of their own role in promoting and driving QI. Commonly, administrative leaders in this phase view QI as clinicians' responsibility and tend to delegate related activities to them. As the first step in the STEEEP Quality Journey, leaders will develop an awareness of the value of QI as a goal shared by all members of the health care organization. This awareness will be fostered by initiatives designed by the organization to educate administrative leaders and board members about QI and its importance to health care. Small and non-hospital-based organizations have a particularly strong need to view QI as a shared imperative because their plans to integrate with other health care institutions will depend on the quality of their processes and outcomes.

Participate in Education Programs Focusing on QI's Application to Health Care

To develop awareness of the importance of establishing a formal QI program, administrative and board leaders should participate in education programs focused on the application of QI to health care. The specific form of these education initiatives will depend on the organization's current culture and the extent to which senior administrators are already committed to QI. For example, education could take the form of presentations by internal or external subject matter experts to administrative and board leaders based on case studies from health care systems positioned at a further phase of the STEEEP Quality Journey. Additional suggestions regarding these presentations are given in Appendix 1.

Education initiatives should also include a more formal course in QI tools and methodologies. At Baylor Scott & White Health (BSWH), STEEEP Academy courses teach administrative and clinician leaders strategies and tools needed to implement QI initiatives. Courses train participants in rapid-cycle QI, Lean thinking, and change management. A more detailed description of STEEEP Academy courses as well as a sample agenda is provided in Appendix 2.

Examples of learning objectives for administrative and board leaders in a QI course include the following:

- The Business Case for Quality (example slides are presented in Appendix 3)
- The Changing Health Care Environment and Its Impact on Quality and Cost
- The Board and Administrative Leader Role in Quality Improvement
- What Leadership Means in the Quality Improvement Context
- How to Identify a Worthwhile Quality Improvement Effort
- Survey of Quality Improvement Tools and Their Use
- Determining What to Measure
- How to Set Stretch Goals
- How to Align Incentives with Quality Improvement
- Change Management Theory and Techniques

For some non-US-based organizations, the challenge is not only to educate leaders but also to effect a change in the culture that includes traditional roles and clinical lines of authority. Board stewardship in initiating and driving this process is critical to its success.

Commit the Organization to Pursuing a Path toward Excellence in Quality and Patient Safety That Will Culminate in Phase 4: Continuous QI

During the Initiation Phase, administrative leaders should commit to establishing a QI program supported by infrastructure, staffing, measurement, and alignment of goals and change that results in improvement throughout the organization. This commitment is crucial for several reasons. First, leadership commitment to quality is the foundation of an organizational culture focused at every level on continuous QI. Second, until board members and senior leaders have committed to QI, costs for establishing QI initiatives are likely to be viewed as expenses for the organization, which may hamper the development and execution of these initiatives. Third, a firm commitment to the QI program from administrative and board leaders will prevent QI from becoming a "fad du jour." It will also help to sustain the organization as it migrates through further phases of the STEEEP Quality Journey and encounters inevitable challenges related to implementation of large-scale change.

Create a Board Resolution That Challenges the Organization to Achieve the Highest Levels of Quality and Patient Safety

Once board members and administrative leaders understand the importance of QI to organizational success and have committed the organization to a QI program, their next step will be to formalize their commitment with a board resolution. An open discussion of organizational success and opportunities for improvement will drive the establishment and adoption of this resolution. At Baylor Health Care System (BHCS), the board established a resolution in 2000 that challenged the organization to achieve the highest levels of patient safety and continuous improvement in the quality of patient care (Appendix 4). This resolution—which was reaffirmed in 2010—laid the groundwork for strategic planning efforts based on health care QI in the ensuing years and ensured that quality was part of the "fabric" of the organization (Ballard et al. 2013). It continues to guide BSWH's strategy today.

Set Macro-Level Goals for the Organization for Quality and Patient Safety

After formalizing the organization's commitment to quality and patient safety, board and administrative leaders will need to establish high-level goals based on this commitment as well as the organization's vision and mission. In addition, so that the organization is positioned to anticipate and act on developments and coming changes in health care policy, organizational quality and safety goals should align with national health care priorities but not be limited only to national efforts.

For example, part of BHCS's STEEEP Quality Journey involved a change to its strategic objectives when, based on both national and local needs, it identified four focus areas it needed to address to realize its vision of being trusted as the best place to give and receive safe, quality, compassionate health care. One of these focus areas was Quality:

- **Quality**: Deliver STEEEP care, supported by education and research
- **People**: Be the best place to work
- **Finance**: Be responsible financial stewards
- **Service**: Serve both our patients and our community

Guided by these four focus areas, the organization developed 10 macro-level goals in 2007. *Quality* goals related to inpatient mortality and performance on Centers for Medicare and Medicaid Services (CMS) Core Measures, *People* goals focused on employee retention, *Finance* goals were based on fiscal operating margin, and *Service* goals focused on patient satisfaction survey scores (Ballard 2003).

These goals support the organization's vision to be the most trusted name in giving and receiving safe, quality, compassionate health care and its mission to serve all people by providing personalized health and wellness through exemplary care, education, and research as a Christian ministry of healing. BHCS also embraced the STEEEP framework in its goals, which lent the Institute of Medicine's (IOM's) widely accepted influence to convey to stakeholders the importance of QI and simultaneously aligned organizational priorities with national health care priorities (Ballard et al. 2013). Although your organization's specific focus areas and goals may differ from the goals in this example, they should incorporate as their foundation your organization's mission and vision as well as national health care quality objectives as encapsulated in the STEEEP framework.

Form a QI Governance Council

A multidisciplinary QI governance council should be formed to plan and implement the QI program, develop and drive organizational health care improvement initiatives, celebrate accomplishments and successes, and guide the organization as it travels through the next phases of its STEEEP Quality Journey. So that QI efforts are driven by all six domains of STEEEP care, council members should include administrative leaders, clinician (physician and nurse) leaders, quality leaders, finance leaders, and patient and family representatives. The council may identify minimal quality measures and benchmarks for those measures, recommend further quality measures as appropriate, and establish a regular frequency of measuring and reporting these data. Board action should empower the QI governance council to prioritize and commit the necessary resources to facilitate the successful implementation of organizational QI initiatives (Ballard, Spreadbury, and Hopkins 2004).

Develop an Organizational QI Entity

The success of your organization's QI program will depend on the infrastructure supporting that program. As part of Phase 1 of the STEEEP Quality Journey, administrative and board leaders should institute a QI entity to develop, implement, and champion initiatives that align with the organization's commitment to quality. In multihospital systems, a QI entity should be established and budgeted for each entity of the organization. In smaller organizations (e.g., a small medical group, a surgical center), the QI resource may consist of a single dedicated person (the QI director).

THE INITIATION PHASE: THE PHYSICIAN AND NURSE LEADERSHIP ROLE IN THE STEEEP QUALITY JOURNEY

Develop an Awareness of the Importance of QI to Your Organization

At the beginning of the STEEEP Quality Journey, many physician and nurse leaders have marginal involvement in QI initiatives because their focus is primarily on clinical delivery and organizational issues. During the Initiation Phase, physician and nurse leaders should expand their awareness of the importance of QI to health care and begin to understand how their leadership in the QI program will facilitate improved clinical processes and outcomes.

Participate in Education Programs Focusing on QI

To enhance their understanding of the importance of QI to the organization, physician and nurse leaders (like administrative and board leaders) should participate in education initiatives designed to foster awareness about the importance of QI to health care. For example, at BSWH, STEEEP Academy courses teach clinician and administrative leaders strategies and tools needed to implement process improvements and other QI initiatives. These courses are described in more detail in Appendix 2. Learning objectives for clinical leaders who participate in a QI course might include the following:

- The Clinical Imperative and Cost-Benefit of Quality
- The Changing Health Care Environment and Its Impact on Quality and Cost
- The Clinician Leader Role in Quality Improvement
- What Clinician Leadership Means in the QI Context
- How to Choose and Manage a Worthwhile QI Effort
- Survey of QI Tools and Their Use
- What to Measure
- How to Set Stretch Goals
- How to Align Incentives with QI
- Change Management Theory and Techniques
- How to Celebrate Change Leading to Improvement and the Need for More and Varied Approaches to Change

Hire/Develop High-Level Clinician Leaders

In Phase 1 of the STEEEP Quality Journey, your organization should hire and develop clinician leaders at the highest levels. Health care delivery organizations should hire clinical leaders such as a chief medical officer and chief nursing officer. In addition, in keeping with the enhanced national focus on population health, these organizations should hire a chief population health officer to lead the development and implementation of population health initiatives across the care continuum. A sample job description for a chief population health officer is included in Appendix 5.

Accountable care organizations (ACOs) should hire a chief medical officer to direct the delivery of the highest-quality, most cost-effective care for the patients served by the ACO. A sample job description for an ACO chief medical officer is included in Appendix 6. Medical groups should also hire a chief medical officer. The multi-specialty medical group affiliated with BSWH, HealthTexas Provider Network (HTPN), employs over 763 practitioners, 633 physicians and 130 physician extenders practicing in 211 care delivery sites in the North Texas area. A sample job description for the HTPN chief medical officer is displayed in Appendix 7.

Assess and Define Your Role in Organizational QI

Clinician leadership is essential for health care organizations to adapt and excel in a continuously evolving health care environment. The combination of medical expertise and leadership ability enables physician and nurse champions to develop health care organizations' capacity to address many of the challenges they face, including the need to make care more STEEEP, as well as the need to improve the patient experience of care, improve the health of populations, and reduce the per capita cost of care in alignment with the Triple Aim framework developed by the Institute for Healthcare Improvement (Berwick, Nolan, and Whittington 2008; Stoller 2009).

One of the first steps in the STEEEP Quality Journey for physician and nurse leaders is an assessment of the roles they play in the organization. Administrative leaders usually think of clinician leaders as valued sources of input on issues of clinical importance. In addition, physician and nurse leaders may play a formal or informal decision-making role through participation on various committees and possibly even membership on the board. All of these roles connect clinician leaders to administrative leaders.

To drive the organization to Phase 2, clinician leaders must be able to balance their role providing clinical care with an ability to work with administrative and quality leaders to implement an organization-wide QI program. This balance can be challenging to maintain for a variety of reasons. For example, clinician leaders may be concerned about time away from direct patient care for attending meetings, participating in conferences, and performing other administrative functions and may wonder how an increased administrative role will have an impact on their long-term career aspirations. In some non-US-based organizations, cultural norms may also present a challenge to the establishment of clinical leadership.

Although many career paths are available to physicians and nurses who choose a leadership role in the STEEEP Quality Journey, the following are the three most typical:

- Remain primarily clinically focused in daily work and participate in QI endeavors as needed
- Maintain an approximately 50%–50% balance between the role of clinician and the role of QI leader
- Become involved in the QI program on a full-time basis

In the first two cases, the organization should establish a process for compensating clinicians for time dedicated to the QI program at the beginning of its journey, which will help to set expectations for future phases. Particularly in small organizations, the shift to an enhanced QI focus is significant for the clinician who practices medicine and serves as the chief medical officer. Becoming a physician leader who focuses on quality may entail important changes in role and daily work.

Take a Leadership Role in Gaining Commitment from Your Board and Administrative Leaders for the QI Program

As noted, administrative leaders usually regard physician and nurse leaders as valued sources of input on issues of clinical importance. Clinician leaders are thus well positioned to encourage board and administrative leaders to create a formal resolution prioritizing quality and patient safety by educating these leaders about clinical processes and outcomes and how these could be improved with an organizational commitment to QI. They can share their own experiences working at the "front lines" of clinical delivery and relate these experiences to issues, trends, and challenges facing the health care environment as a whole.

Participate in QI Council and Programs with Your Nonclinician Colleagues

As noted previously, administrative and board leaders in the Initiation Phase of the STEEEP Quality Journey should form a QI governance council to plan and implement the QI program, drive organizational health care improvement initiatives, and guide the organization as it travels through the next phases of its journey. Physician and nurse leaders—along with administrative (operational and financial) leaders and quality leaders, with selective patient and family participation—should serve as council members to help ensure that QI efforts are driven by all six domains of STEEEP care and to incorporate clinical quality into the organization on a process level. Clinician leaders should also participate in other QI-focused programs with nonclinician colleagues to facilitate a continuous collaboration among clinician, administrative, and quality leaders.

Put in Place a Structure to Provide Leadership to Other Clinicians

Physician and nurse leadership is critical to drive growth and transformation of the organization from the inception of the STEEEP Quality Journey to its culmination in the Continuous QI Phase. Because of the importance of peer leadership to driving clinical efforts to improve quality, many organizations institute a physician and nurse champion program with varying degrees of formal structure and processes. Physician and nurse champions advocate for the QI program, engage their colleagues to undertake and participate in QI efforts, and provide the intellectual capital to teach and launch QI efforts throughout the organization (Ballard, Spreadbury, and Hopkins 2004). In the Initiation Phase of the STEEEP Quality Journey, the work of clinician champions is particularly crucial because, as noted, physicians and nurses at the beginning of the journey may not yet fully appreciate the value of an organization-wide QI program. Physician and nurse champions provide motivation, encouragement, and medical and process expertise to collaboratively design solutions. Clinician champions can be identified in one or several focus areas, including patient safety, clinical preventive services, population health, or medical specialties such as oncology, cardiology, or obstetrics. In complex multihospital systems, hospital-level clinician champions may help to align facility goals and QI efforts with system-wide goals and QI initiatives. In addition, in an era in which health care is increasingly reliant on technology, clinical champions may be needed in areas such as electronic health record design and development, clinical decision support, and implementation support.

Initiate QI Projects within Your Network of Colleagues

As part of their role as advocates for the QI program, physician and nurse leaders will provide leadership for their clinical colleagues. This leadership work, which will require them to initiate and drive QI projects within their network of colleagues, will be different from the clinical work they have performed in the past as well as the collaborative work they are used to undertaking with colleagues. To educate organizational leaders about initiating and implementing QI projects, BSWH uses the STEEEP Academy course described in Appendix 2. Physician and nurse leaders who complete this training are well prepared to identify, plan, and lead QI initiatives in their own departments. Teams of clinicians who initiate QI projects will openly support teamwork and constructive communication leading to continuous QI. They will document the reasons change is needed, collaboratively cause change to happen, and work together to understand the effects of change.

THE INITIATION PHASE: THE ROLE OF QUALITY IMPROVEMENT PROGRAMS AND EXPERTISE IN THE STEEEP HEALTH CARE JOURNEY

Hire/Develop a Chief Quality Officer

At the start of the STEEEP Quality Journey, a chief quality officer (CQO) should be hired to oversee and guide the strategic development of QI initiatives. The CQO will seek to ensure the highest quality of care delivery in accordance with STEEEP aims. He or she may be responsible for the development and implementation of strategies for patient safety, risk management, performance improvement, resource utilization, and care management. In addition, the CQO will be responsible for providing leadership, vision, and strategic direction to conceptualize and implement the most effective infrastructure to drive high-quality outcomes. A sample job description for the CQO is presented in Appendix 8.

Hire/Develop a Director of QI

As part of the Initiation Phase of the STEEEP Quality Journey, administrative and board leaders are challenged to found a QI entity to develop, implement, and champion initiatives to align with the organization's commitment to quality. A few key QI team members will be needed in this entity to coordinate the organization's educational needs and to begin collecting and reporting health care quality data. The first task of quality leaders in the Initiation Phase of the STEEEP Quality Journey is to hire and develop a director of QI to help to guide the organization's new QI function. The director of QI should possess a clinical degree and clinical experience (as a physician, nurse, or pharmacist) with additional experience and training in quality and patient safety and, if possible, an advanced degree such as a master of business administration (MBA) or master of health administration (MHA). The director of QI should report to the organization's chief clinical officer (chief medical officer or chief nursing officer). Among other responsibilities, the director of QI should work with administrative, board, and clinician leaders to develop annual quality goals consistent with the organization's vision and mission and the STEEEP framework. A sample job description for the director of QI is included in Appendix 9.

Particularly in small organizations or organizations where staffing is a challenge, QI may become the responsibility of an administrator with a clinical background (e.g., a former nurse). In such situations, the organization should invest not only in QI training for the director but also in arranging site visits with organizations that are further along in the STEEEP Quality Journey. Such visits will allow the QI director to learn about the resources, processes, and reporting structure of successful QI programs.

Hire/Develop a QI Coordinator

In addition to a QI director, a QI coordinator should be hired or developed. The QI coordinator will work closely with the Data and Analytics Department and will be responsible for preparing and managing data related to regulatory requirements and organizational best care initiatives. The QI coordinator (in addition to the QI director) will serve as a resource for all leaders and employees who develop and implement QI initiatives, including operational leaders and staff. A sample job description for the QI coordinator is presented in Appendix 10.

Approve the Macro-Level Goals Set Prioritized and Agreed to by the Board and Administration

In the Initiation Phase of the STEEEP Quality Journey, board and administrative leaders established macro-level goals based on the organization's commitment to quality as well as the organization's vision and mission. Quality leaders should approve these goals after ensuring they are manageable to achieve and are appropriate to the organization's ability to perform data collection, abstraction, and reporting. The goals and the QI plans supporting their accomplishment will need to be prioritized. To assist in this prioritization, quality leaders will need to contribute their understanding of national and local quality metrics, pay-for-performance metrics, and patient safety metrics that affect the organization. They should remember that the goal of the QI program is also to develop and secure a system with approaches to continuous QI across all lines of activity, including administrative and clinical.

Provide Education Programs to Train Administrative and Clinician Leaders in QI

Few formally established health care QI education programs exist to provide training in QI measurement, tools, and methodologies. For this reason, leaders and other employees who try to establish or engage in QI initiatives often lack the knowledge to do so effectively. As discussed previously, QI education is essential to both administrative and clinician leaders as your organization embarks on its STEEEP Quality Journey. Quality leaders should ensure that QI education—whether on site or off site or online—is provided to these leaders during the Initiation Phase.

The BSWH STEEEP Academy courses provide an example of how to teach administrative and clinician leaders the strategies and tools needed to implement process improvements and other QI initiatives in their departments as well as in the organization as a whole (Appendix 2). Although it is important for these courses to teach general QI methods and tools, courses should also enable students to develop specific QI projects with actionable processes they can perform to achieve particular results.

Often, change management is the most challenging topic for quality leaders to teach and to champion. In each clinical area, quality leaders will be required to advocate for the goals of the QI program and to lead the changes that result from implementation of the program. Initially, these clinical areas may be general (e.g., medicine, surgery), but eventually, they should include each individual specialty program. Depending on the size, impact, and visibility of the specialty program, it may appoint a unique quality leader or may make quality leadership part of the job description of its clinical director.

Establish Ability to Perform Data Collection, Abstraction, and Reporting

Infrastructure for organization-wide QI must include effective systems for measuring and reporting data as required by regulatory agencies as well as for measuring the clinical and financial impacts associated with QI. During the Initiation Phase of the STEEEP Quality Journey, quality leaders should work closely with the Data and Analytics Department to ensure that resources exist for the collection, abstraction, and reporting of data related to overall organizational quality performance as well as the effects of specific QI initiatives. In addition, the development of this capability for the Initiation Phase should be planned in such a way that the tools and infrastructure will extend and scale to the needs of future phases of the journey.

Non-US-based institutions may be constrained by local laws that govern the types of data that can be captured, stored, and analyzed. It may be necessary for these organizations to become "change agents" to encourage modification of these laws for health-care-specific applications that support the provision of high-quality care.

Ensure the Organization Meets Basic Performance Benchmarks for Quality and Patient Safety

Although your organization may operate under different regulations and accrediting entities, we use the Centers for Medicare and Medicare Services (CMS) in the United States as an example because many of the fundamental objectives of CMS reporting are applicable to other settings. At the beginning of the STEEEP Quality Journey, your health care delivery organization should focus on meeting Core Measures, the publicly reported, recommended process-of-care measures developed by CMS and the Joint Commission (Joint Commission 2014.). Core Measures reflect how often a hospital delivers processes of care for high-priority conditions, including acute myocardial infarction, heart failure, community-acquired pneumonia, and surgical infection prevention. In 2003, the Hospital Inpatient Quality Reporting Program began requiring hospitals to submit their Core Measures performance data to CMS, which publicizes it on the Hospital Compare website (Ballard et al. 2013; Medicare.gov 2014).

Because CMS requires hospitals to submit performance data for public reporting, meeting, and eventually exceeding, Core Measures will (1) enable your organization to ensure it has the infrastructure to measure, analyze, and report quality performance data; (2) help your organization to ensure it can deliver important processes of care in a clinically effective manner; and (3) provide a strong foundation from which your organization can launch more complex measurement, analysis, and reporting efforts for the QI program in more advanced phases of the STEEEP Quality Journey.

THE INITIATION PHASE: THE ROLE OF DATA AND ANALYTICS IN THE STEEEP HEALTH CARE JOURNEY

Develop Department and Systems to Measure, Analyze, and Report Organizational Performance as Well as the Effects of Specific QI Initiatives

For a health care delivery organization to achieve STEEEP care and build capacity for QI, it must commit to the development of robust infrastructure. As mentioned earlier, such infrastructure includes effective systems for measuring and reporting the clinical and financial impacts associated with QI.

At the start of the Initiation Phase of the STEEEP Quality Journey, health care data and analytics specialists may have limited ability to extract relevant data and report on quality measures. In addition, data integrity may be contested. To address these challenges, an organizational department should be established to measure, analyze, and report overall system performance as well as the effects of specific QI initiatives. The department should include statisticians, database analysts, and programmers with advanced degrees (e.g., PhD, MBA, master of public administration [MPA], MPH). An example organizational chart for a newly launched analytics department is displayed in Figure 1.2.

In small organizations, QI-related data and analytics are often added to the responsibilities of the Information Technology Department. This is not ideal because employees involved in the QI program should be trained in measurement, analytics, and reporting specific to QI. In addition, their other responsibilities should be backfilled to enable them to develop the skills and knowledge required to support the QI program and to perform effectively in their roles.

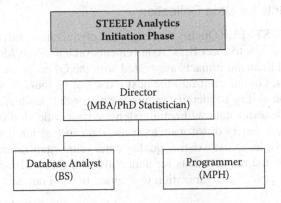

FIGURE 1.2 Example organizational chart for an analytics department.

Develop Capabilities Critical to Organizing, Using, and Reporting Existing Organizational Quality Data

Once an analytics department has been established, it must develop capabilities to organize, use, and report the organization's quality data. These capabilities should include the following:

- Database development and management through advanced programming
- Resources to support the reporting of performance measurement indicators
- Integration of data from multiple sources within the organization as well as state, regional, and national databases for benchmarking purposes
- Management of data from electronic health records and other clinical systems
- Resources to support organization-wide standardized reporting and data requests (Ballard et al. 2013)

Define and Identify Performance Metrics

During the Initiation Phase of the STEEEP Quality Journey, those who specialize in health care data and analytics will learn to define and identify performance metrics relevant to the organization's QI program. Although some of these performance metrics will vary across organizations and countries, the Medicare Value-Based Program provides one example of a performance program whose metrics all health care organizations need to adopt to drive a successful QI program.

The Value-Based Purchasing (VBP) program, which is described in more detail in Appendix 11, is the first of several new pay-for-performance strategies developed by CMS as part of the March 2010 Patient Protection and Affordable Care Act (Patient Protection and Affordable Care Act 2010). The VBP program is designed to promote the triple aim of the US Department of Health and Human Services to improve patient care, improve the health of individuals and communities, and lower health care costs (Berwick, Nolan, and Whittington 2008). VBP presents challenges to health care systems, which could potentially gain or lose millions of dollars a year in reimbursement. For U.S.-based health care organizations, a firm commitment to STEEEP care and to QI beginning in the Initiation Phase of the STEEEP Quality Journey will help to prepare your organization to adopt performance metrics that align with the increased CMS emphasis on quality, patient experience, and efficiency.

Identify Requirements for Data Collection

At the beginning of the STEEEP Quality Journey, your organization will assume a data-driven mentality that will enable it to meet basic requirements such as Core Measures, measure and report the clinical and financial impacts associated with the QI program, and define appropriate performance metrics to launch it into the next phases of its journey. One aspect of a data-driven mentality is the ability to identify requirements for data collection. For example, the monitoring of Core Measures data will entail extensive data collection that may require your organization to engage a variety of software tools and data abstraction resources. As part of its work to develop capabilities to use existing quality data, your organization's data and analytics experts should identify the requirements for data collection that will facilitate success in the Initiation Phase and enable the organization to migrate to the Foundation Building Phase of the journey.

THE INITIATION PHASE: THE ROLE OF REPUTATION AND ACCREDITATION IN THE STEEEP HEALTH CARE JOURNEY

Establish Your Organization with Accrediting Agencies as One That Prioritizes the Delivery of STEEEP Care

In the Initiation Phase of the STEEEP Quality Journey, leaders are establishing and implementing the baseline requirements for a successful quality endeavor. The organization is laying the groundwork to apply for advanced accreditation and seek widespread recognition for its QI program in further phases of the journey. In the Initiation Phase, your organization's most important task related to reputation and accreditation is to establish itself with accrediting agencies as an organization that prioritizes the delivery of STEEEP care. As your organization embarks on further phases of the journey, additional opportunities for accreditation as well as quality awards and recognition will become available.

Important US accrediting agencies include, but are not limited to, the following:

- Accreditation Association for Ambulatory Health Care
- Accreditation Commission for Health Care
- Board of Certification/Accreditation
- Center for Improvement in Healthcare Quality
- Community Health Accreditation Program
- The Compliance Team, "Exemplary Provider Programs"
- Det Norske Veritas (DNV) Healthcare
- Healthcare Facilities Accreditation Program
- Healthcare Quality Association on Accreditation
- The Joint Commission
- National Committee for Quality Assurance
- National Committee for Quality Assurance Patient-Centered Medical Home

Many countries have established similar agencies and commissions to advance the widespread adoption of high standards for patient care and outcomes. The following is a partial list of international health care accreditation organizations:

- Australia: Australian Council on Healthcare Standards International
- Canada: Accreditation Canada
- France: Haute Autorité de Santé
- India: National Accreditation Board for Hospitals and Healthcare Providers
- New Zealand: Quality Health New Zealand
- United Kingdom: QHA Trent Accreditation
- United States: Joint Commission International

The International Society for Quality in Healthcare is the umbrella organization responsible for accrediting the Joint Commission International accreditation scheme in the United States and Accreditation Canada as well as accreditation organizations in the United Kingdom and Australia. The United Kingdom Accreditation Forum is responsible for accreditation schemes in the United Kingdom.

Chapter 2

Phase 2 of the STEEEP Quality Journey
The Foundation Building Phase

INTRODUCTION TO PHASE 2: FOUNDATION BUILDING

Done right, the successful completion of Phase 1 will have provided your organization with a solid foundation for the remainder of its STEEEP (safe, timely, effective, efficient, equitable, and patient centered) Quality Journey. As in any journey, the key to continued success lies in sustaining the initial work as well as building the necessary capacity to move forward.

Because Phase 1 involved significant changes in focus, awareness, culture, and organizational structure, the major challenge for leaders in Phase 2 is to drive against the potential belief that quality can be checked off the "to do" list while focus is redirected to other issues facing the organization. In Phase 2, leaders must sustain a robust commitment to the quality improvement (QI) program, remembering that achieving a culture of continuous QI is not an end point but a journey. They should celebrate the accomplishments of Phase 1 while resolving to intensify their efforts to improve quality throughout the organization.

In addition, the Foundation Building Phase of the STEEEP Quality Journey (Figure 2.1) is characterized by the following elements:

- Continued QI education for leaders
- A robust commitment to measurement of quality, patient safety, and patient experience throughout the organization
- Goal setting commensurate with the organization's commitment to quality, patient safety and patient experience, and continuous striving for greater improvement
- Linking of financial incentives to goal performance
- A more team-based approach to QI throughout the organization
- An evolution of QI solutions from point solutions to more systemic solutions
- The building of a reputation throughout the community that is consistent with the organization's vision, mission, goals, and quality focus

You Are Here

	INITIATION	FOUNDATION BUILDING	OPERATIONALIZING	CONTINUOUS QI
Administration and Governance	• Often unaware of potential benefits of QI • Often do not view QI as their responsibility and instead delegate to clinicians	• Understand the necessity of becoming involved in and providing leadership in QI • Become engaged in QI initiatives	• Directly involved in driving the organization to a culture of QI • Actively measure and reward improvement	• Fully engaged in, and see themselves as accountable for driving QI • Quality is an integral part of their, and the organization's incentive program
Physician and Nurse Leadership	• Often have marginal involvement in QI initiatives • Focus is primarily on clinical delivery and organizational issues	• Active engagement in some QI initiatives • Represent the clinicians and the patient in QI discussions and decisions	• Work together to identify and lead QI initiatives • Become the voice of the patient as well as the clinician	• Fully engaged in QI and drive innovation within their disciplines • Often responsible for engaging their professional communities in QI efforts
Quality Improvement Programs and Expertise	• Limited QI knowledge • Few formally established QI measurement tools and methodologies • Limited or basic safety programs in place	• Pockets of QI expertise • Formal QI structure in place with limited measureable impact • Quality and safety programs across some disciplines and/or facilities • Some best practice initiatives	• Deeper expertise shared across disciplines and/or facilities • Formal structure in place with moderate QI • Organization-wide quality and safety programs	• Established governance and infrastructure for managing and coordinating QI • Formalized QI training for staff at multiple levels • Fully integrated processes, practices, data and analysis • Decision support drives innovation
Data and Analytics	• Little or no ability to extract relevant data and report on quality measures • Data integrity often an issue and a point of debate	• Outcomes/quality measurement and reporting in some areas • Infrastructure capable of extracting data, but with little or no analysis or potential for organizational impact • Quality of data improving and slowly becoming accepted in a number of areas of the organization	• Ability to extract and analyze data to drive QI initiatives • Data integrity no longer an issue and accepted in most areas of the organization	• Established procedures and timelines for data collection and analysis • Development and implementation of data-driven, clinical and operational best practices • Data is used to drive the incentive system for the organization
Reputation/Accreditation	• Basic/minimal accreditation	• Local reputation • Some advanced accreditation	• Regional reputation • Advanced accreditation in several areas	• Nationally recognized as a leader in quality, safety and innovation

FIGURE 2.1 Foundation Building Phase of the STEEEP Quality Journey.

THE FOUNDATION BUILDING PHASE: THE ADMINISTRATION AND GOVERNANCE ROLE IN THE STEEEP QUALITY JOURNEY

Continue to Learn about QI by Participating in Education Programs and Seeking Advanced Leadership Training

In Phase 1 of the STEEEP Quality Journey, administrative and board leaders developed an awareness of the importance of QI to health care by participating in education initiatives deployed by quality leaders from the organization. In Phase 2, administrative and board leaders will continue to participate in the organization's education programs and learn about more advanced QI approaches and techniques in QI; they will also seek advanced leadership training (Appendix 12). Leaders may also wish to visit organizations further along in the STEEEP Quality Journey to gather ideas about how they can continue to transform their organizational culture to one that prioritizes QI as a core value.

As in Phase 1, education initiatives to encourage a continued focus on QI will include presentations to leaders by internal and external subject matter experts. In Phase 2, the audience for such presentations will expand to include upper- and mid-level leadership. More details about the goals of these presentations are described in Appendix 9.

In addition to hosting presentations about the QI program, your organization may wish to hold internal leadership conferences focused on quality. For example, Baylor Scott & White Health (BSWH) educates leaders about quality through quarterly Leadership Development

Institute (LDI) meetings. These meetings, which convene executives, directors, and managers, aim to achieve the following objectives:

- Develop leadership skills so BSWH can achieve its goals
- Align leader competencies with BSWH's values and focus areas
- Improve individual leadership performance
- Rekindle leader passion and commitment
- Raise leadership accountability and consistency
- Enhance employee satisfaction

At LDI meetings, leaders learn about current BSWH performance goals and progress toward meeting those goals. LDI meetings also bring nationally renowned experts from outside the organization to teach and discuss business, leadership, and health care with the intent of providing attendees with a broader perspective regarding QI.

Set Moderately Aggressive Quality, Patient Safety, and Patient Experience Goals

In the Initiation Phase, board and administrative leaders created a formal organizational mandate for quality and safety as well as macro-level goals to support this mandate. During the Foundation Building Phase of the STEEEP Quality Journey, these leaders will further develop the QI program by setting "stretch" goals for quality, patient safety, and patient experience that are commensurate with the vision and mission of the organization. Board and administrative leaders will work to understand what constitutes a reasonable set of goals, the features of appropriate stretch goals, the importance of celebrating changes that lead to improvement, and the negative impact of setting unachievable goals.

Continue to Develop a Culture of QI by Linking Financial Incentives to Quality, Patient Safety, and Patient Experience

In Phase 1, administrative and board leaders established strategic goals for the organization that supported its formal commitment to quality and patient safety. In Phase 2, these leaders, with guidance from clinician and quality leaders, will further drive a culture of QI by aligning leader incentives and performance management programs with these goals, as well as goals related to experience (i.e., patient satisfaction).

At BSWH, the linking of performance management incentives to specific clinical indicators of health care quality began in 2001. In the ensuing years, the organization has more robustly aligned its goal-setting and incentive strategies with its four focus areas (quality, people, finance, and service). Organizational goals in each of the four areas cascade to facilities, departments, and employees at all levels, and a performance award program places a proportion of executive pay "at risk," depending on the extent to which the goals are achieved. The weight applied to each focus area in the performance award program varies according to which areas BSWH identifies as priorities for improvement each year. For example, 70% of the weight in fiscal year 2013 was placed on quality and service goals, commensurate with the board's strong belief that financial success will follow from excellent quality and service (Ballard et al. 2013). A more detailed description of the history of the BSWH performance award program is included in Appendix 14 (Herrin, Nicewander, and Ballard 2008).

Establish a Formal Governance Structure for Quality and Patient Safety

In Phase 1, administrative and board leaders founded a multidisciplinary QI governance council to plan and implement the QI program, develop and drive organizational health care improvement initiatives, and guide the organization through the STEEEP Quality Journey. In Phase 2, the council's role in mandating, coordinating, overseeing, and implementing the QI program will become both more formal and more robust, and its membership will expand to include clinical service lines and business support functions as well as administrative, clinician, quality, and finance leadership, with patient and family involvement, all overseen by board participation. Council members will balance potentially competing interests to develop and implement the QI program in a manner that is appropriate to the knowledge, support, resources, and current quality performance of the organization. The council will also provide guidance to board and administrative leaders as these leaders become more resolute in setting specific performance goals and establishing accountability structures related to these objectives. In particular, the council will focus on the following questions:

- Is the organization following best practices and achieving quality at or exceeding the level of recognized national standards?
- Is the organization providing health care consistent with the STEEEP model?

At BSWH, the STEEEP Governance Council consolidates the efforts of clinical, operational, and financial leadership to ensure that QI efforts encompass all domains of STEEEP care. The structure of the STEEEP Governance Council is depicted in Figure 2.2. The charter for the STEEEP Governance Council is displayed in Appendix 15.

For non-hospital-based organizations, one way to proactively develop relationships with acute care providers as well as to tap into a rich source of knowledge about QI is to reach out to potential partners in the spirit of wanting to improve quality. An understanding of other organizations' QI programs, processes, and measurement and reporting strategies will enable your organization to shape its own program.

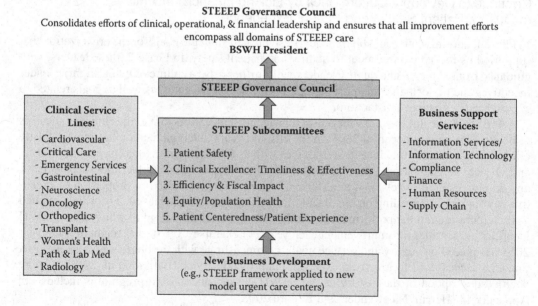

FIGURE 2.2 STEEEP Governance Council structure.

Include Patients and Families in QI Efforts

As your organization progresses through the STEEEP Quality Journey, it will continuously expand its partnership with patients and their families and encourage their role in planning and developing the QI program. In Phase 2 of the journey, including selected patients and families on the QI governance council is one way for your organization to facilitate this partnership and ensure patients are helping to drive STEEEP care.

Drive toward Measurement and Reporting That Will
Highlight Successes and Opportunities

During the Foundation Building Phase of the STEEEP Quality Journey, administrative and board leaders should direct organizational measurement and reporting strategies that will highlight successes of the QI program as well as opportunities for improvement. For example, part of the role of the STEEEP Governance Council is to regularly review metrics associated with STEEEP initiatives and evolve the QI program based on performance across these metrics.

The expenditure for and use of technology to drive this measurement and reporting are critical considerations for organizations in Phase 2 of the STEEEP Quality Journey. In this phase, organizations will typically invest in the use of technology to:

- Gather data
- Analyze data
- Compare performance among different internal and external organizations and standards
- Report outcomes in a way that is specific, meaningful, and impactful to the organization
- Prepare for uses of technology that are more sophisticated in Phases 3 and 4
- Provide systematic approaches to celebrating and sustaining improvement

A common mistake is to underinvest in technology in Phase 2. For example, depending entirely on spreadsheets and manual data entry and reporting may serve the needs of an organization in the beginning of Phase 2 but will hamper continued migration through the STEEEP Quality Journey. Alternatively, spending millions of dollars on highly complex and advanced systems at this stage can result in losing the ability to leverage these systems to meet the needs of Phase 2. As stated, the objective is to select appropriate technology that can be extended and scaled to meet the requirements of each phase.

THE FOUNDATION BUILDING PHASE: THE PHYSICIAN AND NURSE LEADERSHIP ROLE IN THE STEEEP QUALITY JOURNEY

Take a More Public QI Leadership Role

If the Initiation Phase of the STEEEP Quality Journey was about preparation and organizational alignment for the QI program, Phase 2 is about action as well as representation of clinician colleagues and patients in discussions and decision making about QI. During the Foundation Building Phase, physician and nurse leaders will develop a reputation for QI proficiency, both with administrative and quality leaders and with their clinician colleagues. To be perceived as "good-faith brokers," clinician leaders must demonstrate that they possess the technical and organizational skills to successfully drive high-visibility QI efforts that have an impact on a significant portion of the continuum of care.

Engage in Formal Clinician Leadership Training
That Includes Education in Finance

In Phase 1, physician and nurse leaders participated in education initiatives designed to delineate the importance of QI to health care. In Phase 2, to learn to represent their clinician colleagues as well as their patients in QI discussions and decisions and to enhance their understanding of finance in QI, physician and nurse leaders should partake in formal training in leadership knowledge, skills, and techniques. Such training is important for clinician leaders for two reasons: (1) leadership, management, and finance training are not typically included in formal clinical education; and (2) physician and nurse leaders, who are accustomed to "putting the patient first," are ideally positioned to establish and promote team-based QI initiatives and create high-reliability organizations through enhanced management capabilities.

To assess the leadership curriculum elements clinicians would find most effective, your organization may wish to employ a leadership education needs assessment survey. Such a survey will help your organization to identify important educational topics as well as commit the appropriate resources to the training program. An example education needs assessment survey is presented in Appendix 16.

Currently, BSWH provides physician leadership training with an Introductory Physician Leadership Course and Advanced Physician Leadership Training for more experienced physician leaders. These programs are described in more detail in Appendix 17. For nurse leaders, BSWH offers a Nurse Executive Fellowship Program as well as leadership training for front-line nurses through the ASPIRE (Achieving Synergy in Practice through Impact, Relationships, and Evidence) program; these courses are described in Appendix 18. In addition to these programs, BSWH developed in 2014 a STEEEP Academy Leadership Series that includes a course in Clinical Leadership in Quality Improvement and Patient Safety. A list of the topics addressed in this course is presented in Appendix 19.

Collaborate with Administrative and Quality Leaders to Set Annual Quality,
Patient Safety, and Patient Experience Goals for the Organization

In Phase 2, administrative and board leaders are focused on aligning leader incentives and performance management programs with organizational goals related to quality, patient safety, and patient experience. To align these goals and incentives effectively, they will need guidance from both clinician and quality leaders. As physician and nurse leaders recognized in Phase 1, administrative leaders regard them as valued sources of input on issues of clinical importance. To help to drive a successful, sustainable QI program throughout the organization, clinician leaders with input from patients and families need to contribute their unique expertise and perspective to the development of appropriate quality, patient safety and patient experience goals. For non-hospital-based organizations, one reward from having begun conversations with potential partners across the continuum of care is the incentive for your organization to develop and refine its QI program to be prepared for future alliances.

Establish Teams of Individuals from the Entire Organization
Focused on QI and Encourage Active Participation

In the Initiation Phase of the STEEEP Quality Journey, physician and nurse leaders learned to champion the QI program by initiating and driving QI projects within their network of colleagues. In the Foundation Building Phase of the journey, clinician leaders will form multidisciplinary teams of individuals throughout the organization to identify, plan, and lead QI initiatives.

These efforts will require physician and nurse leaders to balance their desire for QI projects to succeed from a strictly clinical perspective with the need for these initiatives to succeed in a comprehensive way that will engage and energize team members to work together to solve more complex problems in the future. Patient and family involvement will help to strengthen and mature these efforts.

To lay the groundwork for future phases of the STEEEP Quality Journey, QI projects in the Foundation Building Phase should meet several criteria. They should be

- **Clinically important**—solving a problem or creating a path for treatment that substantially improves clinical outcomes
- **Scalable**—moving from the pilot department, process, or facility to the organization as a whole
- **Replicable**—using approaches, tools, techniques and skills that can be applied across clinical areas
- **Visible**—facilitating widespread awareness of the clinical impact of the project as well as the clinician role in leading the effort
- **Sustainable**—having support from a structure and resources to enable improvement of outcomes over time
- **Demonstrative of political will**—conveying to the rest of the organization that there is political and organizational power aligned with the QI effort

Evolve QI Focus from Point Solutions to Solutions That Are More Systemic and That Have an Impact on a Larger Portion of the Continuum of Care

In the Initiation Phase of the STEEEP Quality Journey, clinician leaders collaborated with their colleagues to design QI initiatives to solve particular clinical problems or improve quality in a focused area of care. In the Foundation Building Phase, QI initiatives should engage individuals from a wider variety of roles and should generate solutions that are more systemic and that affect a greater portion of the continuum of care. As noted, QI projects in Phase 2 should be clinically important, scalable, replicable, visible, sustainable, and demonstrative of political will. Planning QI initiatives with these features will enable clinician leaders to leverage the effectiveness of their QI efforts and influence a significant part of the organization in preparation for Phase 3: Operationalizing.

Leaders of both hospital- and non-hospital-based organizations in Phase 2 should expand their thinking beyond their organization's walls to include other institutions across the continuum of care. Collaborating with these institutions will enable your organization to expand the scope of its continuum of care and influence the quality of care for patients whenever and wherever they encounter a particular care process.

THE FOUNDATION BUILDING PHASE: THE ROLE OF QUALITY IMPROVEMENT PROGRAMS AND EXPERTISE IN THE STEEEP QUALITY JOURNEY

Collaborate with Administrative and Clinician Leaders to Set Annual Quality, Patient Safety, and Patient Experience Goals for the Organization

In Phase 2, administrative and board leaders are tasked to align leader incentives and employee performance management programs with organizational goals related to quality, patient safety, and patient experience. To accomplish this alignment, they often call on their own experiences in other industries in improving quality and will often depend on guidance from quality and clinician leaders. Quality leaders in particular possess the expertise and experience to help drive the organizational establishment of a variable-pay program. They should provide input regarding the keying of such a program to QI; the definition of stretch goals; and the extent to which compensation should vary depending on organizational achievement of goals across the strategic areas of focus.

Hire/Develop QI and Patient Safety Staff, Preferably with Advanced Degrees or Years of Experience

During the Initiation Phase of the STEEEP Quality Journey, organizational leaders hired a QI director and a QI coordinator and simultaneously began to train administrative and clinician leaders in QI. As a result of these actions, the organization in Phase 2 is likely to be characterized by pockets of QI expertise. Quality and safety programs and best-practice initiatives will probably span disciplines, departments, and facilities, but most have not yet spread across the entire system.

To achieve a more unified and comprehensive organizational approach to QI, quality leaders will need to hire staff and train them in the organization's current portfolio of quality and safety tools and methods as well as its plans to expand and enhance these tools and programs. These staff members should be a resource for all members of the organization who plan, develop, implement, measure, and report the effects of the QI program. By the end of the Foundation Building Phase of the STEEEP Quality Journey, the organization should include a cadre of leaders and practitioners who are both committed to and capable of establishing a continuously more robust QI capacity with quality outcomes consistent with the goals of Phase 2 and eventually Phases 3 and 4. As in Phase 1, administrative and board leadership for QI in Phase 2 will be needed to ensure that staffing costs for the QI program are viewed as crucial elements (i.e., "the way we do business") of the STEEEP Quality Journey and not simply as expenses. The number of staff hired in Phase 2 should be balanced against budgetary and cultural norms and should be consistent both with the current phase and with skill sets that will be needed in subsequent phases. The number of staff hired will depend on the size of the organization, but at a minimum should include administrative support. As the QI resource is brought to appropriate scale for the organization's size, staff members should be added to support each of the following key roles:

- **Department Health Care Improvement Directors**—responsible for quality, patient safety, and patient experience within their departments
- **QI Educators**—responsible for continuous QI, Lean, and other change management education (Appendix 2)
- **Director of Patient Safety**—responsible for patient safety initiatives and for driving a culture of patient safety at the organizational level
- **Director of Patient Experience/Centeredness**—responsible for setting patient experience goals and actions for improvement at the organizational level, with strong patient and family involvement
- **Data Analysts**—responsible for measurement, analysis, and reporting related to quality, patient safety, and patient experience initiatives

A proposed structure for an initial hospital quality department is displayed in Figure 2.3.

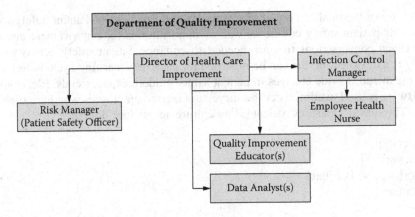

FIGURE 2.3 Proposed structure of a hospital quality department.

Ensure That QI Education Personnel Have Experience in Achieving QI as Well as in Educating Others

During Phase 1 of the STEEEP Quality Journey, quality leaders began to provide education programs to train administrative and clinician leaders in QI, specifically in QI measurement, tools, and methodologies. In Phase 2, these programs will continue to be crucial to building and sustaining an organizational culture of QI. In addition, during the Foundation Building Phase of the STEEEP Quality Journey, quality leaders should ensure that personnel for QI education initiatives have practical experience in achieving QI as well as in educating others. To be successful as instructors, these personnel should have led QI initiatives, implemented the changes required by these initiatives, observed the results of these changes, and learned lessons they can disseminate to students.

Open the Door to Patient and Family Involvement in the QI Program

As your organization progresses toward Phase 4, it will continuously develop its partnership with patients and their families. In Phase 2 of the STEEEP Quality Journey, quality leaders will open the door to patient and family involvement in the QI program in real, useful ways. For example, leaders can gain patient buy-in and support for specific QI initiatives from patient advisors. At BSWH, patient advisors promote organizational change and motivate employees to strive for continuous QI by serving on councils and participating in focus groups and work groups. When the Andrew's Women's Hospital associated with Baylor All Saints Medical Center was built, 20 advisors made recommendations about the design and workflow of the facility. Patient advisors also provide input to improve BSWH's patient safety and infection control strategies.

Deploy a Patient Safety Culture Survey

The Phase 2 organization should prioritize the measurement of quality, patient safety, and patient experience initiatives and outcomes. As part of this focus on measurement, as well as the need to drive the organization toward a culture of patient safety, quality leaders should deploy a patient safety culture survey.

BSWH uses a biennial Survey of the Attitudes and Practices of Patient Safety to identify strengths in its patient safety culture as well as opportunities for improvement and to facilitate data-driven conversations that are needed to enhance patient safety across the system. The survey is a flexible tool that can be modified for each new learning cycle based on nationwide and organization-wide changes in patient safety guidelines and trends. Electronic survey design software is used to administer the survey to targeted employees who have direct patient care roles. The survey measures patient safety culture across four domains:

- Leadership
- Teamwork
- Reporting and Feedback
- Resources

The survey enables data-driven action by reporting answers to questions within these domains at organizational, facility, and unit levels. Examples of survey questions as well as a sample unit-level report are displayed in Appendix 20 (Kennerly et al. 2011).

As part of its efforts to measure and improve patient safety, BSWH also conducts biennial site visits to explore facility effectiveness with regard to patient safety. Site visits are akin to a health "checkup." They promote the spread of evidence-based best practices by allowing leaders to identify patient safety concerns, discover opportunities for shared learning, and ascertain best patient safety practices for dissemination across the organization (Kennerly et al. 2011).

Deploy an Adverse Event Measurement Tool

To reinforce their Phase 2 commitment to quality and patient safety measurement, health care delivery organizations should seek to obtain an objective measure of adverse event (AE) rates across their facilities. With this goal in mind, BSWH adapted and implemented the Global Trigger Tool (GTT) as the Baylor Adverse Event Measurement Tool (BAEMT), a sustainable monitoring tool to characterize AEs for organizational learning. The BAEMT uses a trigger tool methodology to retrospectively identify AEs through standardized review of randomly selected patient records. BSWH expanded the AE data collected to include judgments of preventability, presence on admission, relation to care provided or not provided, and narrative descriptions. These details enable the organization to use the BAEMT data for system-wide learning and improvement and to focus primarily on hospital-acquired AEs (Kennerly et al. 2013).

Improve Equitable Care throughout the Community

During Phase 2 of the STEEEP Quality Journey, your organization should focus on building relationships throughout the community with the goal of linking patients with existing community resources. One way to do this is through charitable care. At HTPN, the community medicine program Baylor Community Care (BCC) aims to improve access to care, provide more equitable care delivery, and produce improved health outcomes for underserved populations in North Texas. Focusing on underserved populations that seek care from BSWH allows us to better meet our mission while also allowing us to develop population health management strategies in a population where we have risk. Effectively managing this population lowers our cost in treating their disease burden. The BCC program consists of eight primary care clinics and innovative support programs targeting unfunded and underfunded patients. BCC utilizes a multidisciplinary team of physicians, nurse practitioners, registered nurses, social workers, and community health workers to operate the following programs:

- A Chronic Disease Management program which provides education to patients with diabetes, heart failure, asthma, and chronic obstructive pulmonary disease (COPD)
- A Behavioral Health program which offers counseling for patients struggling with depression and anxiety
- A Pharmacy program that provides access to affordable prescription medications
- A Specialty Care program which helps connect unfunded patients to specialty physicians and diagnostic testing
- A Home Visit program which provides home-based primary care to home-bound patients
- A Transitional Care program that navigates patients to BCC clinics following discharge from Baylor hospitals

In addition, BSWH employs community health workers to provide culturally and linguistically appropriate health education, navigation, and advocacy services addressing patients' health and social needs. Sample job descriptions for these community health workers are presented in Appendix 21.

THE FOUNDATION BUILDING PHASE: THE ROLE OF DATA AND ANALYTICS IN THE STEEEP QUALITY JOURNEY

Develop Infrastructure for Data Collection and Analysis

In the Initiation Phase of the STEEEP Quality Journey, an organizational department was founded to measure, analyze, and report overall system performance as well as the effects of specific QI initiatives. During the Foundation Building Phase of the journey, an infrastructure for data collection and analysis should be further developed to support measurement, analysis, and reporting related to quality, patient safety, and patient experience initiatives. Data collection processes should be standardized and embedded in the overall processes of the organization. The Data and Analytics Department, with the buy-in and support of finance and operations leaders, must be capable not only of extracting data but also of helping quality leaders to assess the potential of QI initiatives to have widespread organizational impact.

Support Administrative, Clinician, and Quality Leaders in Interpreting Outcomes of QI Initiatives

By the start of Phase 2 of the STEEEP Quality Journey, most senior-level administrative and clinician leaders have been educated in continuous QI, Lean concepts and tools, and change management techniques leading to competent use of these tools to develop and implement QI initiatives (Appendix 2). In Phase 2 of the journey, the Data and Analytics Department will present leaders with robust reports to help them to interpret organizational performance scores as well as the outcomes of quality, patient safety, and patient experience initiatives. Performance should be regularly monitored and benchmarked against national standards and best practices.

For example, the STEEEP Analytics, Measurement, and Reporting Department at BSWH reports monthly to leaders on organizational performance across the Centers for Medicare and Medicaid Services (CMS)/Joint Commission Core Measures. Each facility's "all-or-none" compliance with care bundles for acute myocardial infarction, community-acquired pneumonia, heart failure, and surgical care infection prevention is measured and presented both as a percentage score and in the form of a run chart so that changes in compliance can be assessed over time. Screen shots from a recent report are displayed in Appendix 22.

Provide Measurement Support for the Patient Safety Culture Survey

Quality leaders in Phase 2 of the journey are challenged to deploy a patient safety culture survey to enhance an organizational focus on measurement and to drive the organization toward a culture of patient safety. Measuring the results of this survey and presenting these outcomes for leaders in a meaningful way are top priorities for the Data and Analytics Department in Phase 2. The department should support the QI director and other quality leaders in understanding and interpreting the results of the patient safety culture survey so they can identify best evidence-based practices, close any observed cultural gaps, and improve patient safety across the organization. Patient and family participation is critical to focus and sustainability of these important activities.

Support Organizational Assessment of Adverse Events, Inpatient Mortality, and Patient Satisfaction

In Phase 2 of the STEEEP Quality Journey, quality leaders are tasked to deploy a tool to measure AEs across the health care delivery organization. The Data and Analytics Department will develop methods to support the assessment of these AEs as well as other patient safety metrics, such as hospital-standardized inpatient mortality rates. In addition, the Data and Analytics Department in a US-based health care delivery system will ensure it can support measurement and reporting of patient satisfaction in accordance with HCAHPS (Hospital Consumer Assessment of Healthcare Providers and Services), one of the key factors for determining reimbursement under CMS Value-Based Purchasing (Appendix 11). Measurement and reporting capacity in Phase 2 will enable leaders not only to view the results of measures at the organizational level but also to "drill down" to results at the department, unit, and provider levels. This will allow leaders to both locate opportunities for improvement and accomplish improvement. In addition, measurement and reporting capacity will enable comparison of best practices across different facilities as well as comparison nationally and worldwide and will drive organizational conversations about the importance of "zero defects."

THE FOUNDATION BUILDING PHASE: THE ROLE OF REPUTATION AND ACCREDITATION IN THE STEEEP QUALITY JOURNEY

Build Local Reputation through Community Affiliations, Relationships with Key Stakeholders, and Employee Engagement

In Phase 2 of the STEEEP Quality Journey, your organization should build its local reputation by forging relationships with community organizations that will help it to achieve STEEEP health care as well as to improve the patient experience of care, improve the health of populations, and reduce the per capita cost of care in alignment with the Triple Aim (Berwick, Nolan, and Whittington 2008). The organization should also build relationships with community leaders, including physician and nurse leaders, board members, business leaders, and elected officials.

In addition, it is important to establish relationships with local and regional media outlets and to help them to report on your organization's quality efforts and results.

To help to improve health care throughout its community, BSWH partnered with the city of Dallas and the local community (comprising schools, churches, and local businesses) to develop the Diabetes Health and Wellness Institute (DHWI) at the Juanita J. Craft Recreation Center in the southern sector of Dallas. The DHWI is a health equity model of care that aims to meet the clinical needs of a medically underserved population as well as to provide targeted interventions to promote wellness and behavior modification with the ultimate goal of improving disease management, health, and quality of life (Ballard et al. 2013). The DHWI model of diabetes/chronic disease care is presented in Appendix 23. Through community collaborations similar to the one that fostered the development of the DHWI, your organization should establish itself within the community as an institution that prioritizes quality, patient safety, patient experience, health equity, and health care improvement.

In addition to its relationships with community organizations and leaders, your organization should seek to build its reputation through employee engagement. Employees who understand and are passionate about their organization's mission, vision, values, and goals can act as "ambassadors" for the organization, communicating its commitment to quality throughout the community. BSWH ensures that employees understand its mission, vision, goals, and current progress toward meeting those goals with an ongoing dedication to transparency. In particular, the organization uses learning boards to display a variety of information, including system-wide, facility, and department progress toward meeting goals across the four focus areas of quality, people, finance, and service; current accomplishments and priorities for each department; and current opportunities and ideas for improvement. Many of these boards are visible not only to employees but also to patients, families, and hospital visitors. Learning boards are one way for the organization to document and describe changes and demonstrate its commitment to continuous QI to its employees and the community. Sample learning boards are displayed in Appendix 24.

Identify and Apply for Some Advanced Accreditation

During the Initiation Phase of the STEEEP Quality Journey, your organization focused on achieving basic health care accreditation. In Phase 2 of the journey, it should begin to seek some advanced accreditation in accordance with its size, service line(s), and areas having the most advanced quality processes and outcomes.

Advanced accreditation programs are diverse; they are offered by the Joint Commission and other organizations identified in Chapter 1, as well as by more specialty-focused organizations such as the American College of Surgeons, American Heart Association, American Nurses Credentialing Center, and Society of Thoracic Surgeons. During the Foundation Building Phase, your organization should identify advanced accreditations and certifications that are appropriate for it to seek and apply for these accreditations. These certifications will indicate to health care professionals, patients, and the public that your organization prioritizes STEEEP care; enhance your organization's overall visibility; and foster partnerships with organizations that measure, support, and endorse health care quality.

Chapter 3

Phase 3 of the STEEEP Quality Journey
The Operationalizing Phase

INTRODUCTION TO PHASE 3: OPERATIONALIZING

By Phase 3 of the STEEEP (safe, timely, effective, efficient, equitable, and patient centered) Quality Journey, the Operationalizing Phase (Figure 3.1), all senior-level organizational leaders will be involved in driving the organization to a culture of continuous quality improvement (QI). These leaders will formally have committed to, launched, and laid a solid foundation for the QI program. Now, they will refine the program, frequently reminding themselves and others that QI is not an end point but a journey as well as "the way we do business." After having driven significant improvements in STEEEP care during Phases 1 and 2, leaders need to ensure that the organization does not begin to take these improvements for granted. To attain the aims of Phase 3 and position the organization to migrate to Phase 4, leaders should focus on the following goals:

- Establishment of a culture of QI throughout the organization
- Improved transparency of quality, patient safety, and patient experience data
- Quantitative goal setting based on historical performance and statistical modeling and prediction
- Shared governance to engage all staff in delivering STEEEP care
- Development of a formalized organizational structure for patient safety and patient experience
- Enhancement of data collection, measurement, and reporting capacities
- Building of a regional reputation for delivering STEEEP health care
- Strong patient and family involvement in the QI program

THE OPERATIONALIZING PHASE: THE ADMINISTRATION AND GOVERNANCE ROLE IN THE STEEEP QUALITY JOURNEY

Provide Funding and Support to Achieve Phase 3 Quality, Patient Safety, and Patient Experience Goals and Launch the Organization to Phase 4

As the Operationalizing Phase of the STEEEP Quality Journey commences, all board and senior-level administrative leaders should be directly involved in driving the organization to

You Are Here

	INITIATION	FOUNDATION BUILDING	OPERATIONALIZING	CONTINUOUS QI
Administration and Governance	• Often unaware of potential benefits of QI • Often do not view QI as their responsibility and instead delegate to clinicians	• Understand the necessity of becoming involved in and providing leadership in QI • Become engaged in QI initiatives	• Directly involved in driving the organization to a culture of QI • Actively measure and reward improvement	• Fully engaged in, and see themselves as accountable for driving QI • Quality is an integral part of their, and the organization's incentive program
Physician and Nurse Leadership	• Often have marginal involvement in QI initiatives • Focus is primarily on clinical delivery and organizational issues	• Active engagement in some QI initiatives • Represent the clinicians and the patient in QI discussions and decisions	• Work together to identify and lead QI initiatives • Become the voice of the patient as well as the clinician	• Fully engaged in QI and drive innovation within their disciplines • Often responsible for engaging their professional communities in QI efforts
Quality Improvement Programs and Expertise	• Limited QI knowledge • Few formally established QI measurement tools and methodologies • Limited or basic safety programs in place	• Pockets of QI expertise • Formal QI structure in place with limited measureable impact • Quality and safety programs across some disciplines and/or facilities • Some best practice initiatives	• Deeper expertise shared across disciplines and/or facilities • Formal structure in place with moderate QI • Organization-wide quality and safety programs	• Established governance and infrastructure for managing and coordinating QI • Formalized QI training for staff at multiple levels • Fully integrated processes, practices, data and analysis • Decision support drives innovation
Data and Analytics	• Little or no ability to extract relevant data and report on quality measures • Data integrity often an issue and a point of debate	• Outcomes/quality measurement and reporting in some areas • Infrastructure capable of extracting data, but with little or no analysis or potential for organizational impact • Quality of data improving and slowly becoming accepted in a number of areas of the organization	• Ability to extract and analyze data to drive QI initiatives • Data integrity no longer an issue and accepted in most areas of the organization	• Established procedures and timelines for data collection and analysis • Development and implementation of data-driven, clinical and operational best practices • Data is used to drive the incentive system for the organization
Reputation/Accreditation	• Basic/minimal accreditation	• Local reputation • Some advanced accreditation	• Regional reputation • Advanced accreditation in several areas	• Nationally recognized as a leader in quality, safety and innovation

FIGURE 3.1 Operationalizing Phase of the STEEEP Quality Journey.

a culture of continuous QI. The organizational structure for leading the QI program in this phase will include, but is not necessarily limited to, the following:

- Board members
- Chief executive officer (CEO)
- Chief operating officer
- Chief medical officer
- Chief nursing officer
- Chief financial officer
- Clinical service line chairs
- Leaders from support functions (e.g., human resources, information technology)
- Patient and family leaders to support and drive the culture of continuous QI

Organizational leaders will be required to collaborate to provide funding and support for the QI program to launch the organization to Phase 4 of the STEEEP Quality Journey, when a culture of QI will be embraced and advanced by employees at all levels.

Inculcate and Embed a Culture of Quality, Patient Safety, and Patient Centeredness throughout the Organization

In Phases 1 and 2 of the STEEEP Quality Journey, board and administrative leaders participated in a variety of education initiatives about QI: presentations about the need for QI in health care; programs designed to teach tools and methods for continuous QI, Lean principles, and change management; advanced leadership training; and site visits to health care delivery organizations further along in the STEEEP Quality Journey. As a result of this education, by Phase 3, the principles of change management should be embedded in leadership styles. Meanwhile, administrative leaders will have begun to see tangible results of the QI program, including improvements across measures of care processes, care outcomes, and patient satisfaction. Reports and supporting guidance from the data and analytics department will continue to enable leaders to interpret organizational performance scores as well as the outcomes of quality, patient safety, and patient experience initiatives, and the initial successes created by the QI program should motivate these leaders to inculcate and embed a culture of quality, patient safety, and patient centeredness throughout the organization.

Evaluate and Refine QI Metrics and Commit to a Quantitative Approach to Goal Setting

One way in which board and administrative leaders can embed a culture of quality, patient safety, and patient centeredness throughout the organization is by evaluating and refining goals related to these metrics as well as the role of these goals in the performance award program. During the Foundation Building Phase of the STEEEP Quality Journey, board and administrative leaders linked performance management incentives to outcomes across the organization's strategic areas of focus. They also developed the QI program by setting "stretch" goals for quality, patient safety, and patient experience that were commensurate with the vision and mission of the organization.

In the Operationalizing Phase, board and administrative leaders should have enough historical performance data to refine organizational goals—particularly stretch goals—based on what the organization has already achieved as well as an understanding that QI is a continuously evolving journey. To refine goals appropriately, and to ensure credibility and feasibility for these goals, board and administrative leaders should commit to a quantitative approach to goal setting supported by statistical modeling and prediction. At Baylor Scott & White Health (BSWH), for example, organizational goals are set based on statistical modeling, historical performance, and constraints set by the board and administrative leaders (e.g., the target level for a goal must be at least as high as the previous year's performance). A more detailed description of this quantitative approach to goal setting is included in Appendix 25.

Insist on Transparency of Quality, Patient Safety, and Patient Experience Data to Enable Internal Comparisons and Drive Organization-Wide QI

One primary organizational goal in Phase 2 was a stronger commitment to measurement of quality; in Phase 3, transparency of the outcomes of this measurement will become a top priority. During the Foundation Building Phase of the STEEEP Quality Journey, board and administrative leaders expanded the QI governance council's role in mandating, coordinating, overseeing, and implementing the QI program, and council members were tasked to develop and implement QI efforts in a manner appropriate to the knowledge, support, resources, and current quality performance of the organization. Meanwhile, the data and analytics department began reporting monthly to leaders on organizational performance across quality indicators such as CMS/Joint Commission Core Measures. In the Operationalizing Phase of the journey, these monthly reports will be further expanded and developed to include additional measures of care quality, patient safety, and patient experience and will become accessible to all organizational employees.

At BSWH, the STEEEP Governance Council reviews dozens of performance indicators every month in the STEEEP Care Report. The report currently tracks organizational performance across the following measures:

- CMS/Joint Commission Core Measures (Appendix 22) for acute myocardial infarction, community-acquired pneumonia, heart failure, and surgical care infection prevention
- Inpatient mortality rates related to severe sepsis and intensive care unit (ICU) mechanical ventilation
- 30-day readmission rates for acute myocardial infarction, community-acquired pneumonia, and heart failure
- Adult central-line infections
- Neonatal ICU central-line infections
- Hospital-acquired pressure ulcer prevalence
- Falls and injury falls
- Patient satisfaction at the outpatient, emergency department, and ambulatory surgery levels, as well as Hospital Consumer Assessment of Healthcare Providers and Systems (HCAHPS) scores

This comprehensive quality reporting drives the STEEEP Governance Council's efforts to ensure that QI efforts encompass all domains of STEEEP care and that the organization is achieving quality, patient safety, and patient experience outcomes at or exceeding national benchmarks. Also, because STEEEP Care Reports are accessible to all employees via the organization's intranet, they facilitate internal performance comparisons, an organization-wide commitment to QI, and a shared accountability for the QI program that cascades to staff at all levels. Example graphs from the STEEEP Care Report sections related to inpatient mortality rates and 30-day readmission rates are presented in Appendix 26.

In addition to the STEEEP Care Report, the BSWH CEO dashboard serves as an important information source for board and administrative leaders. The dashboard, which is available on the trustees' intranet portal, depicts quality, finance, and patient satisfaction data at the organization and facility levels. As part of its commitment to making goals and performance across its four strategic areas of focus (quality, people, service, and finance) transparent to all employees, BSWH also displays learning boards throughout its facilities. Data reporting efforts include run charts that enable users to visualize continuous improvement as it occurs over time.

Engage Patients in Discussions and Decisions about the QI Program

One characteristic of a Phase 3 organization is an unwavering focus on the "voice of the patient." Your organization already listens to patients by analyzing its performance across measures of care quality, patient safety, and patient experience; seeking patient and family input on committees dedicated to improving STEEEP care; and asking clinician leaders to serve as patient advocates in decisions about the QI program. During the Operationalizing Phase of the STEEEP Quality Journey, organizational leaders should engage patients even more directly in the QI program. For example, BSWH board and administrative leaders strive to "put a human face" on data related to quality, patient safety, and patient experience by listening to patient stories. A recent board meeting included the Rapid Response Team video, in which a grateful patient and her husband describe how her life was saved by a rapid response team (critical care team) implemented as part of the BSWH's comprehensive patient safety program (Ballard et al. 2013). Patient advisors and patient stories remind leaders and employees of the direct impact of the QI program and help to drive the program's continuous development and refinement.

THE OPERATIONALIZING PHASE: THE PHYSICIAN AND NURSE LEADERSHIP ROLE IN THE STEEEP QUALITY JOURNEY

Drive a Model of Shared Governance throughout the Organization

Physician and nurse leaders will enhance their collaborative QI efforts in Phase 3 by driving a model of shared governance across the organization. Shared governance is a model of co-leadership in which hospital management structures and processes are redesigned to engage all staff in improving health care quality (Casanova 2008). The BSWH Shared Governance Model—originally developed in nursing practice—incorporates the concepts of equity, partnership, accountability, ownership, STEEEP, best care, decision making, patient safety, and evidence-based practice into professional nursing practice (Figure 3.2). It is implemented through a council structure that encompasses unit, service-line, clinician manager, and other councils and enables nurses and other clinicians to act as patient advocates, driving the link between responsibility and authority. Leaders of non-US-based organizations may find themselves constrained by local custom or law and should remember that the most important feature of the model is shared responsibility rather than formal roles.

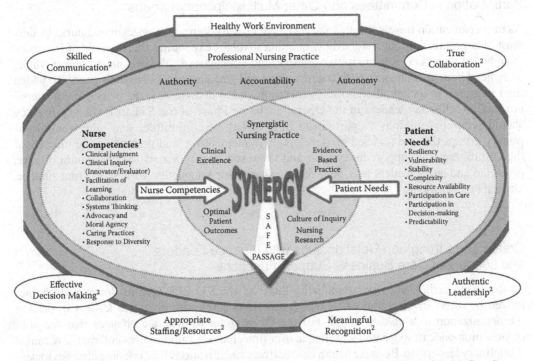

FIGURE 3.2 Baylor Health Care System Professional Nursing Practice Model. (© Baylor Health Care System 2005. Used with permission.[1] Nurse Competencies and Patient Needs from the American Association of Critical Care Nurses Synergy Model for Patient Care. American Association of Critical Care Nurses, 1998. Used with permission.[2] American Association of Critical Care Nurses Standards for Establishing and Sustaining Health Work Environments. American Association of Critical Care Nurses, 2005.)

Leverage the Effectiveness of Your QI Efforts by Expanding Your Focus Organization-Wide

In the Initiation Phase of the STEEEP Quality Journey, clinician leaders designed QI initiatives to solve particular clinical problems; during the Foundation Building Phase, these leaders were challenged to engage individuals from a wider variety of roles in QI efforts and generate solutions designed to affect a greater portion of the continuum of care. Now, as clinicians continue to develop QI projects that are clinically important, scalable, replicable, visible, sustainable, and demonstrative of political will, they should begin to leverage these characteristics across the entire organization by focusing on QI efforts that are organization-wide in scope.

For example, whereas a Phase 2 QI project may have focused on improving care within a particular service line, a Phase 3 QI initiative may engage clinician leaders across several service lines. Clinician leaders of QI projects in Phase 3 should set timelines and document accomplishments and continued opportunities for organizational improvement. Expanding their focus to encompass the entire organization will enable clinician leaders to address QI throughout the continuum of care, drive systemic change, and have an impact on patients regardless of where they encounter a particular care process. Making care more standardized and reliable, improving quality in a systemic manner, and treating each patient encounter as part of an entire experience of care rather than a discrete event will advance the principles of STEEEP health care.

Expand Your Circle of Influence across the Organization through Participation in Committees and Other Multidisciplinary Groups

As the organization travels through the STEEEP Quality Journey, physician and nurse leaders must also progress through a journey, one that involves expanding their sphere of influence from board members, administrative leaders, and colleagues to the organization as a whole. They need both to "manage up" to board leaders and "manage across" to their peers. To widen their influence to include the entire organization and to demonstrate the principles of shared governance, clinician leaders in the Operationalizing Phase of the STEEEP Quality Journey should seek opportunities to participate in a variety of committees and other multidisciplinary groups that are focused on developing, implementing, and measuring the impacts of the QI program. To support integration and improved quality across the continuum of care, physician and nurse leaders may be tasked to share their knowledge with peers from smaller, aligned organizations.

Create and Strengthen Relationships with Finance Leaders and Leaders of Core Business Support Functions

As discussed earlier, the Operationalizing Phase of the STEEEP Quality Journey is characterized by direct involvement of all board and senior-level administrative leaders in driving the organization to a culture of QI. For the QI program to generate changes that are both organization-wide in scope and sustainable over time, the program requires collaborative multidisciplinary leadership. Because health care delivery organizations face ongoing changes to payment systems and increasing adoption of pay-for-performance programs such as Value-Based Purchasing (Appendix 11), they must concentrate on QI efforts that involve both clinician and finance leaders. One crucial goal for physician and nurse leaders in Phase 3, therefore, is to create and strengthen relationships with finance leaders as well as leaders across core business support functions (e.g., human resources, information technology).

Serve as the Voice of the Patient in Discussions and Decisions about QI

Physician and nurse leaders in Phase 3 have learned to represent their colleagues and patients in decisions about the QI program and should now further develop their role as patient advocates, becoming the voice of the patient and guiding the QI program in a manner that is consistent with this dedicated patient focus. Clinician leaders will advocate for enhanced quality of care in terms of care processes, care outcomes, and patient satisfaction to drive STEEEP care and to usher the organization into Phase 4: Continuous QI. Patient and family participation in the QI program can strongly supplement the efforts of clinician leaders. These leaders will involve patients and families in open discussion and communication about STEEEP care supported by continuous QI.

THE OPERATIONALIZING PHASE: THE ROLE OF QUALITY IMPROVEMENT PROGRAMS AND EXPERTISE IN THE STEEEP QUALITY JOURNEY

Make Education in QI Mandatory for All Senior-Level Administrative and Clinician Leaders and Provide QI Training for Additional Leaders

In Phase 3 of the STEEEP Quality Journey, administrative and clinician leaders are focused on implementing change at the organizational level. In addition to senior-level leaders who can plan, implement, measure, and refine QI initiatives at the enterprise level, your organization should educate a variety of QI practitioners who can implement change at the local level. Quality leaders in the Operationalizing Phase of the STEEEP Quality Journey will make QI education mandatory for all administrative and clinician leaders. They will also focus on training midlevel leaders in pragmatic, "frontline" QI. Educational initiatives should focus on the following topics:

- A brief history of QI
- The array of QI tools and how and when to employ them
- How to choose a QI project
- How to find an executive/clinician champion for a QI project

Training in these topics will enable a wider variety of frontline administrative and clinician leaders to identify, plan, and direct QI projects and will facilitate the sharing of QI initiatives across disciplines, facilities, and departments.

Provide Senior-Level Administrative and Clinician Leaders with Continuing QI Education

In Phase 3 of the STEEEP Quality Journey, while your organization trains a wider variety of leaders in the principles and tools of QI, it should also provide continuing education to senior-level leaders who already possess QI expertise as the result of the education initiatives deployed in Phases 1 and 2. This continuing education will underscore the organization's commitment to QI as a journey rather than an end point. This will help to launch the organization into Phase 4, in which QI will be part of its cultural "fabric." Topics for continuing QI education should include the following:

- The impact of health care reform, Value-Based Purchasing, and other trends on health care delivery
- Leading clinical integration through alignment of clinical initiatives with organizational quality and patient safety goals
- Organizing for, mandating, and measuring quality and patient safety
- Promoting standardized, evidence-based best practices
- Dealing with conflict and fostering teamwork
- Using performance feedback reports to drive changes in clinical practice patterns
- Change management versus managing change
- Achieving sustainable quality and patient safety improvement
- The role of shared decision making in STEEEP health care

Dedicate Infrastructure and Resources to an Organization-Wide Patient Safety Department

Your organization has prioritized patient safety since the beginning of its STEEEP Quality Journey and has demonstrated this commitment through its mission, goals, performance award program, robust measurement and reporting strategies, and deployment of a patient safety culture survey and an adverse event (AE) measurement tool. In the Operationalizing Phase of the journey, formal infrastructure and resources should be dedicated to a comprehensive, organization-wide patient safety program. One of the goals of this department will be to develop aggressive action plans to address opportunities identified by patient safety analysis and measurement, including the patient safety culture survey and the AE harm measurement tool. An example organizational chart for a Department of Patient Safety is depicted in Figure 3.3. The goal of this chart is to illustrate how an organization can scale up its infrastructure as it progresses through the phases of the journey. Key areas of focus for the positions are described in Appendix 27.

Dedicate Infrastructure and Resources to an Organization-Wide Patient Experience Department

Like patient safety, patient experience has been a priority for your organization since it first adopted the aims of STEEEP health care in Phase 1. During Phase 2, when quality leaders further advanced patient experience as an organizational objective by collaborating with

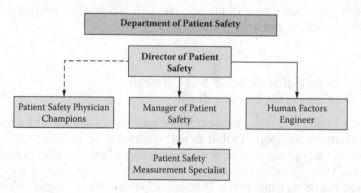

FIGURE 3.3 Example organizational chart for the Department of Patient Safety.

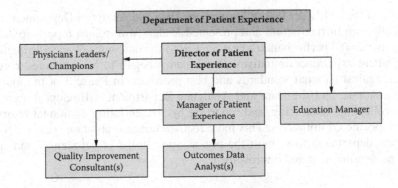

FIGURE 3.4 Example organizational chart for the Department of Patient Experience.

administrative and clinician leaders to set annual quality, safety, and patient experience goals for the organization, and the Data and Analytics Department developed measurement and reporting strategies related to these goals, patient experience evolved to an even more important goal in your organization. As leaders further advance QI initiatives in Phase 3 of the STEEEP Quality Journey, a formalized infrastructure and resources for a patient experience department will be needed to oversee and implement these QI initiatives, as well as to develop patient experience strategies and improve patient experience outcomes at the organizational level. A dedicated patient experience department is also important because of the increased linking of reimbursement to patient satisfaction scores. Leaders of the Patient Experience Department will work to balance the need to provide standardized, evidence-based patient care with the need to develop care plans that are individualized for each patient. An example organizational chart for the Department of Patient Experience is depicted in Figure 3.4; key areas of focus for these positions are described in Appendix 28.

The Patient Experience Department should train organizational staff in the use of a variety of service behaviors to support and facilitate patient-centered care. BSWH promotes the use of eight fundamental service behaviors:

- AIDET (Acknowledgment, Introduction, Duration, Explanation, Thank You)
- Hourly Rounding
- Leader Rounding for Outcomes
- Bedside Shift Report
- Narration of Care
- Managing up
- Open Access
- Care Calls

These behaviors are described in more detail in Appendix 29.

THE OPERATIONALIZING PHASE: THE ROLE OF DATA AND ANALYTICS IN THE STEEEP QUALITY JOURNEY

Enhance Ability to Extract and Analyze Data to Drive QI Initiatives

A primary goal for the Data and Analytics Department during the Operationalizing Phase of the STEEEP Quality Journey is to enhance its capability to extract and analyze data to drive QI initiatives. During Phase 3 of the journey, data integrity should no longer be an issue and should be accepted across most areas of the organization.

In Phase 2 of the STEEEP Quality Journey, the Data and Analytics Department established a data and collection infrastructure and presented leaders with robust reports to help them to interpret organizational performance scores as well as the outcomes of specific quality, patient safety, and patient experience initiatives. Performance began to be monitored regularly and benchmarked against national standards and best practices. In Phase 3 of the journey, these actions will continue, and the Data and Analytics Department will adopt a more proactive approach to collecting, measuring, and reporting by concentrating additional effort on using data to drive specific QI initiatives. This more focused concentration on specific QI initiatives will enable the department to support the organization in the "right sizing" and appropriate prioritizing of measurement and improvement.

Establish Data Governance Policies and Procedures

To operationalize the delivery of STEEEP health care, the Data and Analytics Department should establish organization-wide policies and procedures for data governance. The goal of these policies and procedures will be to drive the standardization and reliability of data collection, measurement, analysis, and reporting. Establishing these data governance policies and procedures involves four main steps: definition, implementation, compliance, and maintenance (Loshin 2010).

Data governance policies and procedures will be specific to your organization, but should at a minimum cover the following areas:

- Information security and data protection
- Accountability for data management
- Accessibility of data based on organizational role and stewardship
- Processes for correcting data issues
- Processes for monitoring compliance with data policies

Employ Reporting Methods That Make Data Interactive, Dynamic, and Drillable

Reporting methods in the Operationalizing Phase of the STEEEP Quality Journey should promote user interaction with data. The Data and Analytics Department should employ effective user interfaces such as dashboards to make data dynamic, drillable (i.e., capable of examination in increasing levels of detail), and easy to visualize. Reporting efforts should include run charts and other tools that allow users to visualize changes in data over time. In addition, the department should train users in these reporting systems and empower them to run their own reports.

The BSWH Blood Utilization Dashboard is an example of a reporting tool that advances STEEEP care by promoting user interaction with data. The dashboard pulls data from multiple sources, including the electronic health record, to depict blood usage levels across various categories (e.g., number of cases, number of units used, average number of units used per case). Dashboard users can filter results according to additional categories, such as surgery date and procedure type, and can drill down to the patient and provider level to understand where, when, and why blood was used. Sample images from a sample blood utilization dashboard are presented in Appendix 30.

Develop Facility and Service-Line Performance Reports

Since the inception of the STEEEP Quality Journey, the Data and Analytics Department has been advancing its ability to present leaders with robust performance reports to aid them in planning, developing, and refining the QI program. The department in Phase 3 should have experience in reporting organizational performance across quality indicators such as CMS/Joint Commission Core Measures and a variety of patient safety and patient experience measures, as well as in benchmarking this performance to national standards.

In Phase 3 of the journey, the Data and Analytics Department should develop analogous performance reports for individual facilities and service lines. These reports will drive organization-wide QI by allowing organizational leaders to drill down to view quality indicator performance at the facility and service-line levels, and by enabling facility and service-line leaders to plan and implement QI initiatives targeted at their entities.

Use Comparative Data to Improve Patient Care

Accountable care organizations in Phase 3 of the STEEEP Quality Journey are well positioned to gain from actionable data to enable continuous quality and efficiency improvement. For example, Baylor Scott & White Quality Alliance (BSWQA), which includes approximately 3,600 physicians, uses Optum One and Explorys to pull data from physician practice electronic health records, hospitals' electronic health records, and claims data from major payers. The diversity of data sources gives physicians and other health care professionals a more complete view of the patient experience and allows them to more effectively plan improvements in care. The system allows them to perform gap analysis, population segmentation, and risk analysis. For example, BSWQA physicians can identify patients at risk because of chronic illnesses and plan efforts to intervene proactively. The system's predictive modeling capabilities also enable BSWQA to identify the sickest patients and those who are at most risk of falling into that category (Raths 2013). A depiction of BSWQA's data architecture and example screen shots from the BSWQA dashboard are displayed in Appendix 31.

THE OPERATIONALIZING PHASE: THE ROLE OF REPUTATION AND ACCREDITATION IN THE STEEEP QUALITY JOURNEY

Build Regional Reputation through Quality Awards and Recognition

During Phase 2 of the STEEEP Quality Journey, your organization built its local and community reputation for high-quality care; in Phase 3, it will expand its reputation for STEEEP care throughout the entire region. By the commencement of Phase 3, your organization will have made significant gains in delivering STEEEP care. One way to publicize these achievements is to apply for regional quality awards and recognition. Examples of such awards in the state of Texas include the Quality Texas Foundation Texas Award for Performance Excellence and the Texas Medical Foundation Texas Hospital Quality Improvement Award. Regardless of whether your organization is selected as a recipient of such an award, the development of an application will enable your leaders to ascertain the progress of the QI program and develop appropriate goals for its future. The journey to an award may be a multiyear journey, but annual feedback reports will be invaluable to its success.

Further Develop Focus on Health Equity

During Phase 2 of the STEEEP Quality Journey, your health care delivery organization began to improve equitable care throughout the community by establishing charitable care clinics and employing community health workers. In Phase 3, your organization will extend this focus on equitable care by concentrating on improving equitable access for vulnerable populations. Your organization may wish to found an Equitable Access Council to oversee this work. In addition to improving access for vulnerable populations, such a council can also help to further develop the organization's strategy with respect to the role of community health workers and other low-cost access options that improve equitable care. Additionally, this council can help navigate these programs through the everchanging governmental and charitable financed programs needed to sustain this work.

Achieve Additional Advanced Accreditation and Certification

Your organization has already tested its ability to deliver STEEEP care by applying for some advanced accreditation and certification. During the Operationalizing Phase of the journey, it will continue to apply for advanced certifications commensurate with its size, service line(s), and areas having the most advanced quality processes and outcomes. Reasons for seeking these advanced national and international accreditations include the following:

- Health care professionals, employees, and patients all want to be associated with industry leaders as well as organizations that prioritize quality, patient safety, and patient experience.
- The rigors of accreditation will provide your organization's leaders with an unbiased evaluation of its QI program.
- Objective, third-party assessments will enable leaders to continuously modify, refine, and expand the QI program.

The patient-centered medical home (PCMH) model also aligns with the aims of Phase 3 of the STEEEP Quality Journey. The PCMH model is an approach to health care delivery system reform that supports the nation's goals of improving quality and coordination of health care across the continuum while reducing costs. HealthTexas Provider Network (HTPN), an affiliate of BSWH, has made significant progress in developing new models of care and is an industry leader in the areas of physician-led culture and patient-centered care. As part of its commitment to STEEEP care, HTPN has obtained National Committee for Quality Assurance (NCQA) recognition for 60 of its primary care clinics (representing 330 providers) as PCMHs. HTPN is now one of the largest networks of NCQA-recognized PCMHs in the nation. This accomplishment has been instrumental in laying a solid foundation for care coordination and population management and has prompted redesign efforts that have improved the patient experience while incorporating key elements of managing patient populations such as pre-visit planning, enhanced patient access, ambulatory care coordination, patient/family activation, disease management, and preventive services.

Chapter 4

Phase 4 of the STEEEP Quality Journey
The Continuous Quality Improvement Phase

INTRODUCTION TO PHASE 4: CONTINUOUS QUALITY IMPROVEMENT

In Phase 4, Continuous Quality Improvement (QI), of the STEEEP (safe, timely, effective, efficient, equitable, and patient centered) Quality Journey, the health care delivery organization's leaders are fully engaged in and see themselves as accountable for driving QI (Figure 4.1). Goals and infrastructure are continuously adapted and refined to enhance quality performance outcomes. Quality, patient safety, and patient experience goals are integrated with organizational behavior and incentives, and QI and innovation are fostered and rewarded.

During the Continuous QI Phase, leaders must foster a culture of continuous QI and drive the organization to sustain Phase 4 results, characteristics, and outcomes. They will focus on the following goals:

- Spread of QI successes by acknowledgment of the people responsible for them
- Hardwiring of variable pay and a quantitative approach to organizational goal setting
- Patient engagement in QI discussions and decisions
- Use of advanced analytic methods to measure the connection among quality, cost, and the organization's financial performance
- Establishment of data-driven clinical and operational best practices to drive to zero defects
- Continuous data-driven, evidence-based refinement of best-care practices
- Utilization of data to take a proactive organizational approach to health care policy changes

In addition, non-hospital-based organizations should assess the level of integration for their QI processes and data both upstream (care given before the patient is treated) and downstream (care given after the patient has been treated) to enable a broader understanding of care quality.

You Are Here

	INITIATION	FOUNDATION BUILDING	OPERATIONALIZING	CONTINUOUS QI
Administration and Governance	• Often unaware of potential benefits of QI • Often do not view QI as their responsibility and instead delegate to clinicians	• Understand the necessity of becoming involved in and providing leadership in QI • Become engaged in QI initiatives	• Directly involved in driving the organization to a culture of QI • Actively measure and reward improvement	• Fully engaged in, and see themselves as accountable for driving QI • Quality is an integral part of their, and the organization's incentive program
Physician and Nurse Leadership	• Often have marginal involvement in QI initiatives • Focus is primarily on clinical delivery and organizational issues	• Active engagement in some QI initiatives • Represent the clinicians and the patient in QI discussions and decisions	• Work together to identify and lead QI initiatives • Become the voice of the patient as well as the clinician	• Fully engaged in QI and drive innovation within their disciplines • Often responsible for engaging their professional communities in QI efforts
Quality Improvement Programs and Expertise	• Limited QI knowledge • Few formally established QI measurement tools and methodologies • Limited or basic safety programs in place	• Pockets of QI expertise • Formal QI structure in place with limited measureable impact • Quality and safety programs across some disciplines and/or facilities • Some best practice initiatives	• Deeper expertise shared across disciplines and/or facilities • Formal structure in place with moderate QI • Organization-wide quality and safety programs	• Established governance and infrastructure for managing and coordinating QI • Formalized QI training for staff at multiple levels • Fully integrated processes, practices, data and analysis • Decision support drives innovation
Data and Analytics	• Little or no ability to extract relevant data and report on quality measures • Data integrity often an issue and a point of debate	• Outcomes/quality measurement and reporting in some areas • Infrastructure capable of extracting data, but with little or no analysis or potential for organizational impact • Quality of data improving and slowly becoming accepted in a number of areas of the organization	• Ability to extract and analyze data to drive QI initiatives • Data integrity no longer an issue and accepted in most areas of the organization	• Established procedures and timelines for data collection and analysis • Development and implementation of data-driven, clinical and operational best practices • Data is used to drive the incentive system for the organization
Reputation/Accreditation	• Basic/minimal accreditation	• Local reputation • Some advanced accreditation	• Regional reputation • Advanced accreditation in several areas	• Nationally recognized as a leader in quality, safety and innovation

FIGURE 4.1 Continuous Quality Improvement Phase of the STEEEP Quality Journey.

THE CONTINUOUS QUALITY IMPROVEMENT PHASE: THE ADMINISTRATION AND GOVERNANCE ROLE IN THE STEEEP QUALITY JOURNEY

Sustain an Organizational Culture That Embraces and Advances Quality, Patient Safety, and Patient Experience at All Levels

Successful organizations not only engage their leaders in a culture of QI but also drive this culture throughout the entire organization. By the start of Phase 4 of the STEEEP Quality Journey, board and administrative leaders have concentrated effort on the QI program for several years and have worked to inculcate and embed a culture of QI throughout the organization. Now, they must sustain the organization's Phase 4 characteristics and results by encouraging and maintaining a focus on QI that is embraced by employees at all levels. Leaders should articulate to employees their understanding that QI is not an end point but a journey, and that the organization must constantly strive to improve STEEEP care.

Spread QI Successes by Acknowledging Achievements and the People Responsible for Them

To sustain an organizational culture of STEEEP care, board and administrative leaders should acknowledge and reward the successes the organization has achieved so far. As a result of organizational efforts to provide widespread education about QI, innovative ideas for improving STEEEP care should have emerged by Phase 4 from a variety of departments, teams, and employees. Your organization can use a variety of recognition and reward strategies to acknowledge these successes.

For example, Baylor Scott & White Health (BSWH) presents monthly Service Excellence Awards and quarterly Chief Executive Officer (CEO) Awards of Excellence to individual employees who have advanced STEEEP care in their units, departments, or facilities. Employees who win these awards are formally recognized by leaders and provided with a monetary reward; in addition, their role in promoting QI is publicized via the organization's intranet, learning boards, and other sources.

For BSWH, the annual Bill Aston Quality Improvement Summit provides a larger forum for celebrating and rewarding QI successes and sharing QI initiatives and processes throughout the organization. To be eligible for an award, a team must be nominated by its hospital or facility for its work to establish and maintain improvement consistent with STEEEP aims and the organization's strategic areas of focus (quality, people, service, and finance). Winning teams are formally recognized by the CEO and other senior-level leaders at the QI Summit. The Bill Aston Quality Improvement Summit encourages the spread of successful QI initiatives and processes.

Promote Accountability for QI by Hardwiring Variable Pay and a Quantitative Approach to Organizational Goal Setting

Previously in the STEEEP Quality Journey, board and administrative leaders linked performance management incentives to outcomes across the organization's strategic areas of focus and embraced a quantitative approach to goal setting supported by statistical modeling and prediction. In Phase 4, the organization's performance award program and quantitative approach to goal setting should be hardwired as part of its commitment to continuous QI and its expectation that all leaders will be accountable for QI. To further promote a sense of shared accountability for QI, board and administrative leaders should make performance award program measurements at the organizational and facility level transparent to all employees (Appendix 32) and should empower organizational committees not only to monitor but also to take action to correct insufficiencies in quality, patient safety, and patient experience performance. Hardwiring the connection between financial incentives and quality performance will strengthen the connection among the elements of STEEEP care.

Continuously Drive a Care Partnership with Patients and Families

Administrative leaders in Phase 4 of the STEEEP Quality Journey will continuously identify, develop, and implement strategies to engage patients and families in QI. In this phase of the journey, patients not only will help to design QI initiatives but also will engage as partners in their own care. For example, several BSWH facilities offer a previsit patient orientation to involve patients and families in their care plan. The orientation provides patients and families with information about how they can address questions and concerns; introduces them to specific care initiatives (e.g., rapid response team, hand washing); or teaches them about facility support services, such as nurse navigation. In addition, patients and families are offered a tour of the facility that is customized to their care plan. Patient orientation, education, and tours represent initiatives that improve STEEEP care while fostering patient and family involvement in care.

Accountable care organizations in this phase of the STEEEP Quality Journey will foster a more robust care partnership with patients and families through enhanced care coordination. Their patients will benefit from an integrated system of care and referrals as well as evidence-based processes, protocols, and clinical pathways created by physicians to standardize care more effectively. Accountable care organizations also offer advanced electronic information integration to improve patient care across settings. All of these features of accountable care organizations drive STEEEP care while involving patients and families more strongly in their own care.

Measure and Publicize the Link between Quality and Cost

By Phase 4 of the STEEEP Quality Journey, the organization will be able to demonstrate a link between improving quality and managing costs, and finance leaders will be powerful advocates for the QI program. Pay-for-performance programs such as Value-Based Purchasing (Appendix 11), ongoing changes to the Medicare payment system, and the elimination of payment for "never events" (egregious medical errors) all represent examples of the increasingly strong connection between quality and cost in the minds of patients, payers, and policy makers. To recognize and reinforce this link between quality and finance, board and administrative leaders in Phase 4 should support the development of advanced analytic capabilities to measure the business and financial impact of QI initiatives.

THE CONTINUOUS QUALITY IMPROVEMENT PHASE: THE PHYSICIAN AND NURSE LEADERSHIP ROLE IN THE STEEEP QUALITY JOURNEY

Continuously Drive Organizational Goal Setting with Your Clinical Expertise, QI Experience, and Role as Patient Advocate

Physician and nurse leaders in Phase 4 have long-standing experience collaborating with administrative and quality leaders to set annual quality, patient safety, and patient experience goals for the organization. During the Continuous QI Phase of the STEEEP Quality Journey, the goal-setting process and performance award program will be hardwired as part of the organization's ongoing commitment to QI. Physician and nurse leaders should be completely engaged in the organization's goal-setting process, using their clinical expertise, their experience with QI as fostered by the organization's education programs, and their unique role as patient advocates to continuously recommend, implement, and drive STEEEP care.

Drive Innovation within Your Discipline, Both Inside and Outside the Organization

In Phase 3 of the STEEEP Quality Journey, physician and nurse leaders expanded their circle of influence across the organization through participation in committees and other multidisciplinary groups. Now, they will sustain their engagement with these groups and will expand their influence even further, engaging their professional communities in QI efforts. For example, clinician leaders may disseminate best practices through peer-reviewed medical and health care journals. This will enable the organization to drive widespread innovation; enhance its reputation for STEEEP care among health care professionals; and facilitate the delivery of STEEEP care throughout the community, region, nation, and world.

Continuously Define, Refine, and Implement Evidence-Based Best Practices throughout the Organization

Phase 4 organizations use data and evidence to continuously develop, refine, and implement best clinical and operational practices. In the Continuous QI Phase of the journey, each organizational goal related to quality, patient safety, and patient experience should be supported by a portfolio of evidence-based best practices and decision support tools (e.g., order sets, checklists, diagnostic support tools) that can be deployed by physician and nurse leaders to enhance evidence-based best practice. Evidence-based best practices should be continuously refined as new data become available. Standardization and outcome improvements should also be tracked and reported.

For example, the World Health Organization (WHO) launched the Safe Surgery Saves Lives (SSSL) Initiative in 2007 to reduce variation in surgical care (Haynes et al. 2009). The SSSL Checklist targets important safety processes, including effective teamwork and communication, safe anesthesia practices, and prevention of surgical infection. Baylor Health Care System (BHCS) piloted the checklist at eight hospitals and, in a sample of 3,733 surgical cases, demonstrated that the checklist reduced inpatient complications from 11.0% to 7.0% ($p = .003$) and 30-day mortality rates from 1.5% to 0.8% ($p < .001$) (Ballard et al. 2013). As a result, the organization developed a resolution to fully implement the WHO SSSL Checklist beginning in 2009. The SSSL Checklist, displayed in Appendix 33, provides an example of how continuous QI can be used to help drive toward zero defects.

Establish and Lead Service-Line Quality Improvement Councils to Foster a Stronger Connection among the Elements of STEEEP Care

In Phase 3 of the STEEEP Quality Journey, physician and nurse leaders advanced collaboration between themselves and their nonclinician colleagues by driving a model of shared governance, expanding their influence through participation in committees and other multidisciplinary groups and creating and strengthening relationships with finance leaders and leaders of core business support functions. To drive the organization during the Continuous QI Phase of the STEEEP Quality Journey, clinician leaders should establish and lead service-line QI councils and initiatives.

By Phase 4 of the journey, all senior-level leaders—including service-line chairs—will be directly involved in driving the QI program, and QI initiatives should engage clinician leaders across multiple service lines. Establishing and leading formal QI councils at the service-line level will enable physician and nurse leaders to address QI throughout the continuum of care and drive systemic change that has an impact on patients across the entire organization. For example, the BSWH Cardiovascular Surgery Quality Council provides a formal organizational structure and oversight for activities and QI initiatives related to cardiovascular and cardiothoracic surgery. To advance system-wide QI that is evidence based, aligned, cohesive and comprehensive, this council reports to the organization's chief quality officer and chief medical officer. The Cardiovascular Surgery Quality Council's charter is presented in Appendix 34.

THE CONTINUOUS QUALITY IMPROVEMENT PHASE: THE ROLE OF QUALITY IMPROVEMENT PROGRAMS AND EXPERTISE IN THE STEEEP QUALITY JOURNEY

Continuously Refine Organizational Goals and the QI Program to Enable the Organization to Reach and Exceed Performance Established by National Benchmarks

Quality leaders have been collaborating with administrative and clinician leaders since the Foundation Building Phase of the STEEEP Quality Journey to set annual quality, patient safety, and patient experience goals for the organization. In Phase 4, the goal-setting process and performance award program will be hardwired and quality leaders will be completely engaged in the goal-setting process. They will use their expertise to provide specific input regarding the keying of the organization's performance award program to QI as well as to drive the continuous refinement of the QI program to enable the organization to reach and exceed performance established by national benchmarks.

Continuously Develop Infrastructure for Coordinating and Managing the QI Program

As the organization evolves and becomes larger and more complex, its QI staff should be continuously developed and expanded. The senior quality leader who is responsible for quality, patient safety, and patient experience should continue to serve a significant role on the senior leadership team. In addition, all clinical departments should have quality leaders as well as clinician leaders who champion quality. These leaders will coordinate and manage the QI program throughout the organization and advance a culture that embraces and advances continuous QI as well as STEEEP care.

Provide Formal QI Training for Staff at Multiple Levels

By the start of Phase 4 of the STEEEP Quality Journey, quality leaders have made QI education mandatory for all senior-level administrative and clinician leaders, provided senior-level leaders with continuing QI education, and provided QI education to a variety of practitioners who can implement change at the local level. Quality leaders will sustain these actions while ensuring that all clinician, nurse, and pharmacist leaders as well as all administrative managers above a certain level possess an understanding of QI, Lean thinking, and change management (Appendix 2). Providing formal QI education to staff across disciplines and leadership levels will support the organization's efforts to embed QI in its culture.

Spread Successful QI Initiatives by Fostering and Rewarding Improvement

Leaders in Phase 4 should foster continuous QI by formally recognizing the successes the organization has achieved so far. At BSWH, the annual Bill Aston Quality Improvement Summit celebrates and rewards QI successes and spreads QI initiatives and processes across the organization. Formerly the chair of the Baylor University Medical Center Board of Trustees, the late Bill Aston drafted the 2000 board resolution to prioritize quality and patient safety (Appendix 4) and was one of BSWH's original champions of QI (Ballard et al. 2013). Four QI case studies originating from the Bill Aston Quality Improvement Summit are presented in Appendix 35. The case studies describe QI initiatives that improved care by

- Decreasing ventilator mortality in the intensive care unit
- Decreasing 30-day readmission rates for patients with acute myocardial infarction, community-acquired pneumonia, and heart failure
- Improving laboratory and emergency department specimen turnaround times
- Training providers in electronic health record use

Utilize Decision Support Tools to Drive Innovation and STEEEP Care

In the Continuous QI Phase of the STEEEP Quality Journey, leaders will use decision support tools, both electronic and paper based, to plan, implement, and continuously refine the QI program. Clinical decision support enables data-driven decisions by providing leaders with information that is specific to facilities and patients. It includes a variety of tools, such as clinical guidelines, condition-specific order sets, electronic alerts and reminders, diagnostic support tools, drillable data reports, and focused patient data reports and summaries. Next, several decision support tools are described in more detail. The use of such tools enables leaders to be proactive and innovative in their approach to the QI program and helps them to drive STEEEP care by reducing errors, adverse events (AEs), and complications; enhancing the effectiveness and efficiency of care; and improving the patient experience of care.

THE CONTINUOUS QUALITY IMPROVEMENT PHASE: THE ROLE OF DATA AND ANALYTICS IN THE STEEEP QUALITY JOURNEY

Support the Establishment and Maintenance of Data-Driven Clinical and Operational Best Practices

As in previous phases of the STEEEP Quality Journey, the primary function of the Data and Analytics Department will be to measure, analyze, and report overall system performance as well as the effects of specific QI initiatives. By the start of Phase 4 of the journey, data collection processes should be standardized throughout the organization, and the Data and Analytics Department should be capable of providing robust support and education to leaders as they interpret reports to assess the impact of the QI program. The Continuous QI Phase of the journey will be characterized by an ongoing data-driven approach to establishing and maintaining clinical and operational best practices, directing the incentive system for the organization, and measuring organizational performance as it relates to policy initiatives such as Value-Based Purchasing. Data will be used to compare organizational practices to best practices nationally and worldwide and drive the organization toward zero defects.

At BSWH, a variety of reporting tools advance STEEEP care and its associated data-driven clinical and operational best practices. For example, organizational leaders seek to reduce and eliminate nonbeneficial variation in care by analyzing costs of care across DRGs (diagnosis-related groups). Using these reports, leaders can identify services provided to all patients, reduce unnecessary variation in care, reduce the risk of complications, and make care more reliable and more STEEEP.

Use Data to Promote a Proactive Organizational Approach to Health Care QI That Is Policy Driven

By Phase 4 of the STEEEP Quality Journey, organizational leaders will be able to use data to take a proactive approach to changes in health care policy. For example, BSWH continuously ascertains organizational readiness for Centers for Medicare and Medicaid Services (CMS) Electronic Health Record Incentive Programs that govern payment procedures related to the "meaningful use" of health information technology (CMS 2014). To be eligible for a financial incentive, health care delivery organizations must show that they are meaningfully using their electronic health records by meeting thresholds across a number of objectives. The eQuality Measure and Meaningful Use Dashboard displays organizational performance across 39 measures, includes linked definitions, and enables users to drill down by facility to monitor ongoing progress and improve performance during each reporting period.

Develop Resources and Technology to Utilize Large Data Sets and Integrate Data from Multiple Sources

Measuring and improving care entails the assimilation of data from a multitude of sources. During Phase 4 of the STEEEP Quality Journey, your organization should develop resources and technology to utilize and integrate large data sets and ascertain the additive impact of diverse variables on care. At BSWH, the Data Mining Laboratory (DML) applies advanced computational methods and software to integrate data from multiple organizational and regional databases. A recent retrospective study supported by the DML analyzed data from 2,027 trauma patients over a year following index admission to a level I trauma center to identify risk factors for readmission. Data were collected from a regional database encompassing readmissions across 54 hospitals in 49 counties. BSWH leaders will use the findings of this study to improve STEEEP care by developing interventions to reduce the readmission rate (Appendix 36). The DML supports organizational efforts to compare clinical and operational practices with best practices across the region, nation, and world, as well as to drive the organization toward zero defects.

Develop Advanced Analytic Capabilities That Include Financial-Modeling Abilities

During the Continuous QI Phase of the STEEEP Quality Journey, the organization should develop and deploy advanced analytic capabilities that include reporting and analysis as follows:

- Statistical business charts for monitoring, risk adjustment, and statistical techniques to determine outliers and cost opportunities
- Risk modeling to identify specific interventions to improve STEEEP care
- Financial modeling to improve care quality and reduce costs (e.g., the determination of cost variability across DRGs)
- Leveraging of publicly available data (e.g., Hospital Compare, CMS, Texas Health Care Information Collection, Leapfrog, other business coalitions and health care delivery systems)
- Business intelligence reporting to analyze data generated as part of business operations, assess historical operational performance, and predict the consequences of future decisions

THE CONTINUOUS QUALITY IMPROVEMENT PHASE: THE ROLE OF REPUTATION AND ACCREDITATION IN THE STEEEP QUALITY JOURNEY

Apply for National Quality Awards and Recognition

To constantly drive STEEEP health care, Phase 4 organizations must sustain their passion for quality as a top priority. By the Continuous QI Phase of the journey, your organization will have achieved returns on its QI investment that include improvements in processes of care, clinical outcomes, patient experience, and financial impacts. Publicizing its achievements and commitment to quality will allow it to build its national reputation and attract and retain the best people and partner organizations:

- Clinicians who aspire to practice in Phase 4 environments
- Employees who want to work for organizations that advance STEEEP health care
- Referring physicians who want the best care with the fewest complications for their patients
- Patients who seek, based on information available on the Internet, the best care available
- Payers that want to partner with high-quality organizations to which employers and consumers demand access

As in Phase 3, your organization will apply for quality awards to publicize its commitment to STEEEP care. In Phase 4, it will expand its application efforts to include national awards such as the National Institute of Standards and Technology Baldrige National Quality Award and the National Quality Forum National Healthcare Quality Award. Although winning an award is the goal of these application efforts, many QI initiatives are multiyear endeavors that will be facilitated by annual feedback reports to identify opportunities and actions for improvement. In addition to quality awards, accreditation and certification are important in Phase 4 of the STEEEP Quality Journey. Accreditation will include prominent certifications such as Magnet recognition from the American Nurses Credentialing Center.

Tell the Story of Your Organization's STEEEP Quality Journey

Applying for national quality awards and accreditation will help your organization to tell its story: how it began the STEEEP Quality Journey, its progression through the journey, where it stands in comparison to other organizations, and how it plans to continue the journey. Telling your own story will allow your organization to celebrate its accomplishments so far while recognizing that continuous QI and a commitment to STEEEP care are part of an ongoing, ever-advancing journey.

SUMMARY

This guide has covered a variety of strategies and approaches to launching and sustaining a QI program and continuously improving STEEEP care throughout your organization. It has described the phases, roles, and tasks that drive the STEEEP Quality Journey. Specific tools, methods, presentations, and case studies to support your organization's QI program follow in the Appendixes. The most important lessons of the STEEEP Quality Journey are as follows:

- QI is a journey, not an end point.
- A successful QI program requires participation at all levels of the organization, from board members to frontline clinicians, with patient and family involvement.
- Each phase of the STEEEP Quality Journey builds on the groundwork laid by the previous phases; organizational leaders should make decisions about the QI program with future phases of the journey in mind.
- Measuring quality within the four walls of your institution is not enough; comprehensive QI across the entire continuum of care is required for your organization to best serve its patients as well as the priorities established by partners, payers, and policy makers.

APPENDIXES: TOOLS, METHODS, AND CASE STUDIES TO OPERATIONALIZE THE STEEEP QUALITY JOURNEY

Now that you understand the different phases and organizational roles that drive the STEEEP Quality Journey, you should begin to develop specific tools and methods for your organization's QI program. The following appendixes provide a basic set of presentations, tools, methods, and case studies that together can serve as a "starter kit" to enable your organization to commence the STEEEP Quality Journey. Although each of the items is presented individually, it is important to remember that the QI program is not a collection of isolated methods and tools but instead is a continuously evolving journey and process. Also, although the content of these appendixes is current as of the date of publication, refinement and improvement of these tools are ongoing. BSWH welcomes the opportunity to provide updated tools and methods to readers:

David J. Ballard, MD, PhD, MSPH, FACP
Chief Quality Officer, Baylor Scott & White Health
8080 North Central Expressway, Suite 900, LB 77
Dallas, TX 75206
info@steeepglobal.com
www.STEEEPGobalInstitute.com

Appendix 1: The Initial Presentations to Board and Administrative Leaders to Gain a Commitment to Quality

WHO?

Who will most effectively influence your audience and make them want to commit to an organizational quality improvement (QI) program? In some instances, the answer is someone from outside the organization (e.g., an external health care expert, a leader from another respected health care organization). In other cases, the answer is someone from within your own organization (e.g., the chief executive officer, chief medical officer, chief nursing officer).

WHAT?

An initial presentation to board members about the importance of establishing a QI program might aim to achieve the following objectives:

- Encourage awareness of the issues, trends, and challenges facing health care
- Ask board members to assess what the organization's competition, top performers, and communities are doing to improve health care quality
- Establish a business case for quality
- Invite board members to create an initial vision, goals, and a mandate for QI; assign organizational responsibility and staffing for implementation of a QI program; and set initial quality goals for the organization

HOW?

The most effective way to influence the target audience is to provide the necessary information, customizing the messages and the opportunity and threat to the organization and giving the audience an opportunity to discuss the pros and cons of establishing a QI program. The presentation should also recommend a process for leaders not only to commit now but also to continuously renew that commitment throughout the STEEEP Quality Journey.

In addition to presentations to key stakeholders, one-on-one meetings should be held with leaders whose support is critical to the adoption of the QI program. These meetings should focus on the aspects of the QI program that are most important to that leader (e.g., the chief executive officer will be concerned about clinical outcomes and patient experience as well as financial impacts and organizational reputation).

Appendix 2: Quality Improvement Training—STEEEP Academy

INTRODUCTION

BSWH is committed to providing administrative, physician, nurse, and other health care leaders with the knowledge and tools needed to deliver STEEEP care. The organization founded the "ABC Baylor" course in 2004 to teach internal leaders skills and techniques needed to lead quality improvement (QI) efforts. In 2011, recognizing the importance of the course to STEEEP care, organizational leaders incorporated the course into the STEEEP Academy, which provides external physicians, nurses, and administrators with tools for cultural and process change to facilitate QI in a variety of health care delivery settings.

STEEEP Academy courses teach rapid-cycle QI, which is based on the simple Plan–Do–Check–Act (PDCA) model:

- **Plan** a change aimed at quality improvement
- **Do** the tasks required to implement the change, preferably on a small scale
- **Check** the results of the change
- **Act** to adopt or abandon the change

In addition, STEEEP Academy courses incorporate a variety of other process improvement methodologies and tools with a focus on creating a culture of continuous QI including the following:

METHODOLOGIES

- Define, Measure, Analyze, Improve, Control (DMAIC) and Six Sigma: Reducing variation and defects
- Lean thinking: Emphasizing the voice of the customer, adding value, eliminating waste, and improving flow
- Change management

TOOLS AND TECHNIQUES

- Strengths, weaknesses, opportunities, and threats (SWOT) analysis
- Value stream maps

- Fishbone diagrams
- Gap analysis
- Visual management
- Cost-benefit analysis
- Pareto analysis
- Run charts

STEEEP ACADEMY SAMPLE COURSE AGENDA

Day 1

- Commitment to Quality
- Issues Facing Health Care
- Systems Thinking
- Course Case Study Round #1—Evaluating Current State
- Defining Performance Improvement
- Understanding Lean and Six Sigma
- PDCA and DMAIC Models for Improvement
- Project Prioritization and Selection
- Scoping the Project
- Developing a Problem Statement
- Developing an Aim Statement
- Establishing a Team
- Effective Team Meetings
- Leading Through Change
- Communication During Change

Day 2

- Understanding Variation
- Impact of Human Factors on Variation
- Success Story—Quality Improvement Project
- Mapping the Process
- SIPOC (suppliers, inputs, process, outputs, and customers), Value Stream Map, Flow Chart, Functional Deployment Chart
- Methods and Techniques to Identify Issues
- Conducting a Waste Walk
- Drilling Down to Root Causes
- Correlation vs. Causation
- 5 Whys
- Fishbone Diagram and Root Cause Tree
- Failure Modes and Effects Analysis
- Establishing a Measurement System
- Identifying and Selecting Measures
- Developing a Data Collection Plan
- Evaluating the Measurement System

Day 3

- Patient Centered Care
- Cost of Quality
- Prioritizing Issues
- Multi-voting
- Interrelationship Diagraph
- Impact and Frequency Matrix
- Pareto Chart
- Developing Solutions that Focus Around STEEEP
- Innovation
- 8 Wastes
- 5S
- Standard Work
- Visual Management
- Mistake Proofing
- Stop the Line
- Push vs. Pull Systems
- Course Case Study Round #2—Improving Efficiency
- Evaluating & Prioritizing Solutions
- Benefit and Effort Matrix
- XY Matrix
- Developing Action Plans
- Teach Back Exercise

Day 4

- Impact of Social Media
- Types of Data
- Properly Displaying and Sharing Data
- Bar Chart
- Scatter Diagram
- Histogram
- Run Charts
- Control Charts
- Closing the Project Cycle
- Abandoning, Adapting or Adopting
- Communication Boards and Huddles
- Recognizing Performance
- Continuous Improvement and Spread
- Course Case Study Round #3—Kaizen Event
- Project Review
- Teach Back Exercise

Day 5

- Course Review—Jeopardy Game
- Project Review
- Wrap-up, Next Steps, and Adjourn

Appendix 3: Example Presentation Slides: Building a Business Case for Quality

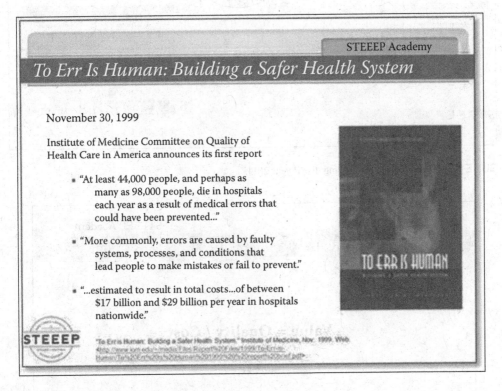

FIGURE A3.1 To Err Is Human: Building a Safer Health System.

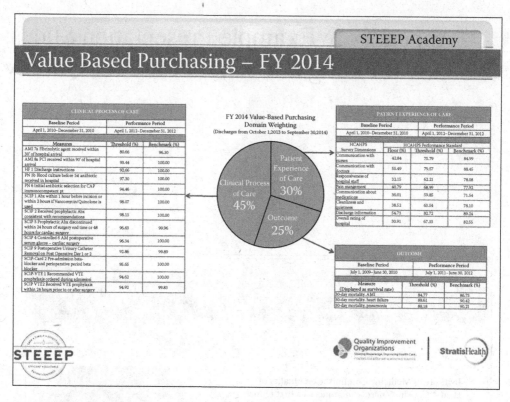

FIGURE A3.2 Value-Based Purchasing: fiscal year 2014.

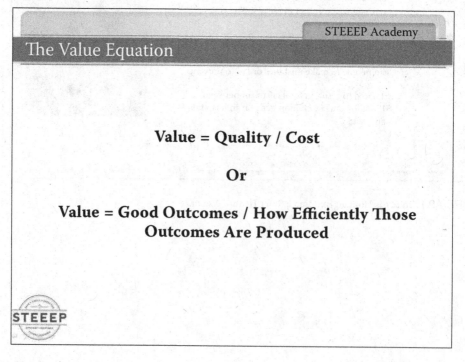

FIGURE A3.3 The value equation.

Appendix 4: Board of Trustees Resolution

RESOLUTION
BOARD OF TRUSTEES
BAYLOR HEALTH CARE SYSTEM
September 26, 2000

WHEREAS, Baylor Health Care System's Vision Statement includes "the most trusted source of comprehensive health services"; and

WHEREAS, Baylor Health Care System's Mission Statement includes "serve all people through exemplary health care"; and

WHEREAS, one of the primary responsibilities we have as Trustees is continuous improvements in quality patient care and safety; and

WHEREAS, maintaining the status quo or achieving quality and safety levels only equal to or slightly better than national, regional, or local norms is not compatible with the BHCS Vision and Mission Statements; and

WHEREAS, regulatory and legislative changes and a growing number of more informed patients support better quality patient care and safety;

THEREFORE, BE IT RESOLVED, that the Board of Trustees of Baylor Health Care System hereby challenges itself and everyone involved in providing health care throughout the system to give patient safety and continuous improvement in the quality of patient care the highest priority in the planning, budgeting and execution of all activities in order to achieve significant, demonstrable and measurable positive improvement in the quality of patient care and safety; and

FURTHER RESOLVED, that the Board requests that periodic reports be made to the Board on planning, budgeting, execution and results of activities to improve patient safety and quality of patient care in Baylor Health Care System.

E. R. Brooks, Chairman
Board of Trustees

September 26, 2000

FIGURE A4.1 Board of Trustees resolution.

Appendix 5: Sample Job Description for Chief Population Health Officer

The Chief Population Health Officer (CPHO) will be an innovative and progressive leader accountable for leading the vision, development, and implementation of progressive population health initiatives throughout the system and across the care continuum of Baylor Scott and White Health (BSWH). This position represents a new way of thinking and a shift from fee-for-service to value-based models of care. The CPHO will have to navigate this transition and balance the risks, sensitivities, and complexities of leading these types of efforts across a complex and evolving organization that spans multiple regions. The CPHO will establish organizational focus, coordinate available resources, align educational activities and policies and procedures, and lead the development of new models of care.

EDUCATION REQUIRED

- M.D. or D.O.
- Active medical license
- Master's degree preferred
- Experience as a leader in population health, patient-centered medical home, and administration
- 10 years of experience preferred
- Experience working in a complex, matrixed health care system

JOB FUNCTIONS

- The CPHO will champion population health strategies throughout the system and enhance internal capabilities to ensure an industry-leading strategy is achieved. The CPHO will establish close collaborative relationships with internal stakeholders to ensure alignment as reimbursement models continue to evolve. This individual will develop new external relationships and partnerships and mature existing external relationships and partnerships at local, regional, state, and national levels in support of BSWH overall accountable care strategy.
- The CPHO will be a population health thought leader and subject matter expert who is abreast of industry trends and economic, legislative, and technological advances/ changes.

- The CPHO will partner with key executives and clinical leaders to design and shape market-specific strategies, as well as coordinate internal resources vital to the operationalization of these initiatives. The CPHO will serve as a key system representative and spokesperson with external stakeholders (payers, employer contracts, community leaders, governmental advocacy, and public health policy).
- The CPHO will be part of the senior leadership team, be visible to the Board of Trustees, and lead initiatives that will impact the organization in a meaningful way. Population health is a key strategic imperative.
- The CPHO must be comfortable working in a highly matrixed environment and have the ability to drive change without solid lines of accountability.
- The CPHO will partner closely with senior leaders throughout the system to ensure a full continuum of population health services that meet the demands of the markets and communities served by BSWH.
- The CPHO will work closely with the Scott & White Health Plan (SWHP) leadership to leverage the existing strengths and capabilities of the health plan and position SWHP to meet the evolving demands of health care reform and industry trends.
- The CPHO will lead the integration of the hospital-based care coordination and social work staff with ambulatory-based care management staff while creating new models of care coordination that support population health management.
- The CPHO will develop and monitor key population health performance indicators and work with executive and operational leadership to enhance them.
- The CPHO will oversee the BSWH equitable access initiatives including government programs like the Medicaid 1115 Waiver.
- The CPHO will lead the STEEEP Analytics team, which is responsible for internal reporting for performance improvement including incentive programs, as well as external reporting including regulatory, public transparency, risk stratification of defined populations, and clinical efficiency analytics including identification of nonbeneficial variation.
- The CPHO will function as a key system representative with both internal and external stakeholders and will be accountable for the vision, strategy, and development of capabilities critical to the success of a population health strategy.

SKILLS AND ATTRIBUTES

- A genuine commitment to the Mission of the organization and personal and professional values consistent with the values espoused by Baylor Scott & White Health.
- The ability to take calculated risks to serve as a catalyst for change while engendering confidence and trust in doing things differently.
- The ability to work well and build trust with both independent and employed physicians.
- The ability to build teams, garner support, and champion a vision and mission across a broad and complex multi-region environment.
- The ability to leverage pre-existing relationships and build new collaborative partnerships with both internal and external stakeholders.
- The ability to be an inclusive consensus builder and collaborator who is comfortable working in a highly matrixed setting.

- The ability to plan, organize, and prioritize resources and manage multiple high-priority demands to meet the organization's goals and objectives.
- The ability to be a progressive leader with a "finger on the pulse" of the industry, and the foresight and intuition to keep BSWH abreast of change and at the forefront of population health strategies.

The CPHO's scope will include the population health management work that is being developed in BSWH's clinically integrated organization, Baylor Scott & White Quality Alliance (BSWQA). Since the BSWQA's work will be critical to the overall BSWH population health strategy, the CPHO will also serve as the chief medical officer for the BSWQA. As both roles grow, there may be a need to hire a separate chief medical officer. The CPHO will continue to relate to this work at least through a matrixed leadership role.

Appendix 6: Sample Job Description for an Accountable Care Organization Chief Medical Officer

The Chief Medical Officer (CMO) role of the Baylor Scott & White Quality Alliance (BSWQA) directs the delivery of the highest-quality, most cost-effective care for the patients served by the BSWQA. The CMO will report to and work directly with the President of BSWQA, as well as collaborate with the entire executive team, the Chief Operating Officer, the senior administration of Baylor Scott & White Health, and the Board of Managers of BSWQA to advance the strategic objectives of the BSWQA and to attain both short- and long-term objectives of the organization.

JOB FUNCTIONS

- Serves as a vital member of the senior management team and prepares reports for the President and in turn the Board of Managers of BSWQA that reflect the progress and success of the organization as it pertains to the quality, cost of care, and clinical integration for the patients served.
- Executes and achieves the strategic goals and objectives to position BSWQA for long-term success, consistent with BSWH's established mission, and promotes the role of BSWQA and BSWH to the public, health care organizations, professional associations, and purchasers of health care services.
- Integrates the BSWH Chronic Disease and Transitional Care initiatives to assure that the overlapping processes are harmonized with activities of BSWQA to avoid redundancy and optimize and manage these activities in the most efficient manner.
- Furnishes medical direction for Baylor Physician Services (BPS) as it engages in care coordination of patients in HealthTexas Provider Network (HTPN) and BSWQA contracted populations.
- Leads the BSWQA medical directors in their efforts to facilitate the work of the BSWQA Best Care Committee and sub-committees. Integrates that work with the Best Care Committee of HTPN, BSWH service lines, and in turn with the BSWH STEEEP Governance Council. Within that structure, coordinates the work of specialty subcommittees of the BSWQA Best Care Committee to develop order sets and care paths and protocols for both inpatient and outpatient processes of care.

- Expands the function and capability of patient-centered medical homes by both employed and independent physicians participating in BSWQA.
- Collaborates closely with BSWQA information technology and Analytics leadership to assure adequate measurement of quality and clinical integration initiatives and their use for reporting and performance management.
- Works with the Chair of the BSWQA Finance Committee in advising the BSWH Office of Managed Care Contracting, particularly to serve as BQA input on clinical performance contractual criteria.
- Maintains current knowledge of integrated delivery network and accountable care organization functions through reading literature; attending workshops, seminars, and conferences; and participating in professional organizations.

Appendix 7: Sample Job Description for a Medical Group Chief Medical Officer

(a) Define Quality Improvement (QI) project(s) and develop quality protocols and metrics.

(b) Coordinate the nature and extent of QI and Best Care projects with the President of the Employer, the Chairman of Employer's Board of Directors and the Chairman of Employer's Best Care Committee.

(c) Implement Best Care projects within Physician's clinical or administrative sphere of influence with Employer.

(d) Engage in rapid-cycle Plan-Do-Study-Act (PDSA) activities.

(e) Report results of PDSA activities to Best Care Committee.

(f) Represent HealthTexas Provider Network (HTPN) on the BSWH North, Chief Medical Officer Council.

(g) Read current QI Literature.

(h) Leverage the knowledge and techniques of smaller projects into Employer-wide projects, as well as QI/Best Care efforts of BSWH.

(i) Work synergistically with other quality-impacting efforts of the Employer, such as electronic health record (EHR) development.

(j) Develop content for HTPN ambulatory EHR.

(k) Improve Adult Preventative Health Services scores.

(l) Improve diabetes scores of patients for quality initiative targets set for all of HTPN.

(m) Improve the care of Asthmatic patients as measured by the quality initiative targets set for all of HTPN.

(n) Improve care of coronary artery disease patients as measured by the quality initiative targets as set for all of HTPN.

(o) Lead a disease management strategy for HTPN, focusing on Patient-Centered Medical Home and use of the Care Coordination Model.

(p) Develop care coordination and care gap management within practice sites and between hospitals to home.

(q) Lead heart failure/coronary artery disease/pneumonia improvement projects and other projects related to transitional care.

(r) Improve access for patients through development of same-day appointment plans, after hours/extended hours care in HTPN clinics, and by partnering with other organizations to provide after hours and weekend care.

(s) Lead effort to improve "keepage" of patients within BSWH from a quality improvement and patient safety aspect.

(t) Work with data analytics to develop protocols (both primary care and specialty care) and metrics to improve patient care as well as value (increase quality, decrease cost) for the health care system.

(u) Work with data analytics to develop patient work lists for physicians and care coordination to focus and improve patient care.

(v) Serve as member of multiple committees including as Chair of the Best Care Committee and member of the Ambulatory Electronic Health Record Committee.

(w) Manage and oversee HTPN Physician Champions.

(x) Oversee Physician Work Flow redesign project.

(y) Communicate with HTPN physicians through writing (email, etc), video, and in-person presentations regarding HTPN Best Care initiatives.

(z) Represent HTPN on the BSWH North Physician Leadership Council.

Appendix 8: Sample Job Description for Chief Quality Officer

ACCOUNTABILITIES AND RESPONSIBILITIES

- Assesses, develops, and implements policies, procedures, and infrastructure, from a systemic viewpoint, that demonstrate improved outcomes in safety and quality programs.
- Provides the leadership framework for planning, directing, coordinating, and improving services by the Quality Management Department that are responsive to the needs of the organization.
- Develops, recommends, and monitors key quality performance indicators for the organization.
- Directs the Quality Management Program.
- Plans, organizes, and directs strategic plans for continuous compliance with external accreditation standards (e.g., Joint Commission, CMS).
- Promotes a status of continuous survey readiness for accreditation surveys conducted by The Joint Commission.
- Maintains oversight responsibility for all performance improvement activities conducted throughout the organization.
- Supports and implements patient safety and other safety practices as appropriate.
- Supports development of and participation in research.
- Facilitates department budget preparation and administration. Promotes sound fiscal management and adherence to budgetary standards through the budget review process.
- Reviews operational results, as scheduled.
- Provides leadership support in the communication and incorporation of the mission and vision Statements.
- Provides support in developing and implementing long-range strategic and cooperation plans that support the vision and mission statements.
- Functions as a member of the System Executive Committee and other committees as appropriate.
- Establishes policies and procedures for the Department and works with appropriate governing bodies for approval of said policies and procedures.
- Reviews the operational performance towards achieving the established objectives and the specific accountabilities.
- Communicates frequently with leadership through regular reports, meetings, etc. to ensure effective coordination of hospital activities.
- Recruits, retains, and evaluates the staff necessary to implement the goals, objectives, and responsibilities of the Quality Management Department.

- Establishes linkages with outside agencies/departments in order to enhance and support the quality programs.
- Provides guidance and collaborates with Management staff in assessing the need for training of staff and leadership in quality improvement concepts and the development and implementation of performance initiatives.
- Maintains a collaborative relationship with all levels of staff throughout the organization, to promote an open line of communication for problem resolution and quality care.
- Demonstrates a broad understanding of, and takes personal responsibility for, key financial indicators.
- Supports management, development and effective use of human resource capital.
- Provides communication to staff on a regular basis regarding education requirements for compliance with accreditation standards, and utilizes performance management as a developmental tool.
- Develops strategies and guides the organization in setting directions and seeking further opportunities based on clear values, high performance expectations, and internal/external customer focus.
- Adheres to the organization's Code of Conduct at all times and serves as a role model to all staff.
- Maintains professional competencies by attending educational programs, participating in professional organizations, reading of professional journals, or performing other appropriate activities.
- Performs other duties and related functions as required.

SKILLS

- Team building including the possession of good interpersonal skills, the ability to persuade others to change their minds or behavior, and the ability to work effectively with all levels of an organization.
- Self-directed, thorough, and committed to a team approach.
- Solid analytical skills and the ability to make quick, effective decisions under pressure.
- High energy, with the capacity to successfully manage many projects/responsibilities simultaneously.
- Strong resource management skills, including the ability to effectively manage time, finances, materials, facilities, and personnel.
- Personal and professional values such as integrity, honesty, and loyalty.
- Ability to serve as a key member of the senior leadership team and contribute broadly at the executive level.

GOALS AND OBJECTIVES

As CQO, your first 12 to 18 months will include the following objectives:

- Partner with senior management and become fully integrated into the leadership team. Be perceived as a solid team player who has credibility and integrity, and contributes broadly as a health care executive subject-matter leader.
- Evaluate the current staff, establish an appropriate organizational structure, and hire, mentor, and develop the team as needed.

- Work collaboratively and build relationships across the organization, including the regional leaders, physician leaders, and the C-suite executive team.
- Strengthen physician relationships, build trust, and gain physician engagement for enhanced adoption of clinical and financial systems as they relate to quality management.
- Provide the leadership to execute on the system quality, operational, and capital budgets, consistent with agreed upon timelines and objectives.

Appendix 9: Sample Job Description: Director of Quality Improvement

- Leads the quality improvement (QI)/performance improvement operations across the organization. The results of this accountability would be
  - Demonstration of improvements in the facility's evidence-based care measures, to achieve safe, timely, efficient, effective, equitable, and patient-centered care in all care settings.
  - Consultation as the methodological expert in process improvement tools and methods.
  - Identification and communication of specific health care processes based on the results of hospital-based health care improvement that have the potential to advance best care.
  - Collaboration with patient safety and risk management functions.
  - Demonstration of the ability to facilitate improvement activities designed to improve patient outcomes, reduce costs, and improve patient and family perceptions about the quality and value of services.
  - Increase in external and national recognition for best practices in clinical care provided.
- Trains and educates organizations in QI techniques and tools, such as continuous QI activities, failure modes and effects analysis, and data collection tools.
- Facilitates inspections conducted by external agencies, which may include but are not limited to the Joint Commission and the Food and Drug Administration, and prepares the necessary responses to those inspections.

Appendix 10: Sample Job Description: Quality Improvement Coordinator

- Prepares and manages statistical data through the extraction of relevant material as related to core measures, best care initiatives, reliability audits, investigations/inspections, patients, and other information as required by the department. The collection or tracking of information may include, but is not limited to, that relating to the Code of Federal Regulations, Food and Drug Administration, and Joint Commission.
- Maintains communication with regulatory and accreditation agencies to remain abreast of requirements, deadlines, and anticipated changes.

Appendix 11: Centers for Medicare and Medicaid Services Value-Based Purchasing

In federal fiscal year 2013, the Centers for Medicare and Medicaid Services (CMS) tied reimbursement to performance in the areas of clinical processes of care and patient experience through Value-Based Purchasing. The clinical measures include, for example, the rates of health care-associated infections. Patient experience (satisfaction) is measured by the Hospital Consumer Assessment of Healthcare Providers and Systems (HCAHPS), which measures patients' perceptions of how well their health care needs were met.

In federal fiscal year 2014, CMS added a third domain for patient outcome measures. This includes 30-day mortality rates for deaths that occur within 30 days after their release from the hospital among patients with heart attack, heart failure, and pneumonia.

In federal fiscal year 2015, a Healthcare Research and Quality composite measure, the patient safety indicator (PSI-90), will be added to the program. In addition, CMS will add a fourth domain for efficiency, which will measure Medicare spending per beneficiary (see Figure A 11.1).

Value-Based Purchasing

FY 2014 Value-Based Purchasing Domain Weighting (Discharges from October 1, 2013, to September 30, 2014)

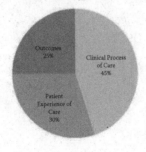

FY 2015 Value-Based Purchasing Domain Weighting (Discharges from October 1, 2014, to Septembers 30, 2015)

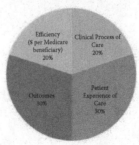

FIGURE A11.1 Value-Based Purchasing.

Appendix 12: Advanced Quality Improvement Training for Board Members

In 2014, Baylor Scott & White Health (BSWH) developed the STEEEP Academy Leadership Series (Figure A12.1) to prepare health care leaders with the necessary knowledge and strategies to lead and sustain meaningful improvements in health care quality and patient safety. One of the courses targeted board members of health care organizations; topics of the course included the following:

- Challenges in health care delivery, including accountable care, population health, and value-based purchasing
- The role of the board in quality improvement and patient safety
- Strategic goal setting for the organization
- Understanding health care quality data
- The quality performance measurement report (exercise)
  - Reviewing quality and safety data
  - Evaluating improvement strategies and progress
- Establishment of executive accountability
- Next steps in your organization's STEEEP Quality Journey

FIGURE A12.1 STEEEP Academy Leadership Series: Board Governance in Quality and Patient Safety.

Appendix 13: Presentations to Leaders to Sustain a Commitment to Quality

WHO?

Administrative and board leaders are often bombarded with presentations of "the next big thing" and therefore approach such presentations with some skepticism about the results the proposed program will achieve. To rise above the noise, quality proponents in Phase 2 should include a wider range of individuals, such as hospital chief executive officers (for multihospital organizations), clinicians who are known to the board but who have not previously presented to them about quality improvement (QI), and staff from the "front line" of care delivery who can offer first-hand knowledge about ways the QI program is having an impact on patients, families, and staff.

WHAT?

In the early Phase 2 environment, presentations to board members and administrative leaders about the QI program should cover several points:

- Background about what the organization's quality program had originally **planned to accomplish**
- Results depicting the **actual accomplishments** of the organization's quality program so far
- Things the organization's quality program has **started to accomplish** and needs to focus on in Phase 2
- **Specific actions** required to expand the Phase 1 accomplishments and drive the organization into Phase 2
- **Specific items needed** from the board to support this migration to Phase 2

Appendix 14: Aligning Incentives with Organizational Goals

INTRODUCTION

When Baylor Health Care System (BHCS) leaders first added clinical indicators to the organization's performance award program, they linked incentives to the meeting or exceeding of performance targets for Centers for Medicare and Medicaid Services (CMS)/Joint Commission Core Measures for acute myocardial infarction care. This was the first time in the nearly 20-year history of the performance award program that senior leader and manager performance was evaluated based not solely on fiscal indicators but also on clinical quality. In the following year, the measures included in the quality index of the performance award program were expanded to include Core Measures for community-acquired pneumonia, and in 2004 and 2005, respectively, Core Measures for heart failure and surgical infection prevention were added to the program. In subsequent years, measures included in the quality index have changed to reflect the evolving focus of organizational improvement efforts; for example, the quality index now includes requirements for specific reductions in measures of in-hospital mortality.

PHILOSOPHY OF VARIABLE PAY

Baylor Scott & White Health (BSWH) offers competitive base salaries for executives that approximate the 50th percentile of salary ranges for similar positions in similar organizations. With the additional compensation associated with the performance award program, when the organization meets its goals in the areas of quality, people, service, and finance, executive salaries stand at the 75th percentile or above, depending on whether the goal is met or exceeded. The board's philosophy is to reward employees when the organization meets its goals while maintaining executive salaries as a variable cost if the organization fails to achieve its goals. This approach to compensation has helped BSWH to better allocate its cost for salaries and reward higher performance while challenging itself to appropriately evaluate goal achievement. An additional strength of the BSWH approach to variable executive compensation is that incentives are discretionary rather than expected as an entitlement (Ballard et al. 2013).

STRUCTURAL SUPPORT FOR GOAL SETTING

The organization founded a multidisciplinary Goal Setting Subcommittee in 2009, composed of stakeholders in each of the four areas of focus. Currently, the subcommittee identifies the goals to be included in the performance award program for any given year and makes recommendations to senior leaders and the board about goals and metrics. For example, with the introduction of the CMS Hospital Value-Based Purchasing program—which uses HCAHPS (Hospital Consumer Assessment of Healthcare Providers and Systems) patient satisfaction surveys to determine which providers should be rewarded and which penalized for their performance—the subcommittee recommended adopting the HCAHPS patient survey measures for organizational goals to better align them with the national performance metrics (Ballard et al. 2013).

Appendix 15: BSWH STEEEP Governance Council Charter

1. Purpose
   a. The purpose of the STEEEP Governance Council ("Council") is to provide oversight, set strategy and direction, and effectively prioritize those initiatives and operational functions that fall within the six domains of STEEEP health care (Safety, Timeliness, Effectiveness, Efficiency, Equitable, Patient-Centered) and assign primary responsibility for those initiatives crossing multiple domains.
2. Membership
   a. The Council is chaired by the BSWH Chief Quality Officer. The membership of this committee may change by consensus of the voting members should the need arise.
   b. Decision making within the committee is driven by a quorum of the voting members. A simple majority of voting members will constitute a quorum to approve decisions and minutes.
   c. The Council may form subcommittees, approve charters for these subcommittees and delegate authority to them as appropriate. Initial designated subcommittees include:
      i. Patient Safety,
      ii. Clinical Effectiveness (Timeliness and Effectiveness domains),
      iii. Efficiency and Fiscal Impact,
      iv. Population Health and Equity,
      v. Patient Centeredness/Patient Experience,
   d. Initial designated aligned entities include:
      i. BSWH STEEEP Measurement, Reporting and Analytics group,
      ii. BSWH STEEEP Academy training resource,
      iii. BSWH Clinical Service Lines.
   e. To carry out its duties the Council shall have the authority to engage and obtain advice and support internally or externally as it deems necessary.
3. Council Membership
   The Council shall be made up of the positions outlined below.
   a. Voting Members:
      i. Chief Medical Officer
      ii. Chief Nursing Officer
      iii. President
      iv. BSWH Chief Financial Officer
      v. HTPN President, Chair of Board and Chief Clinical Officer
      vi. Scott & White Physician Board Chair
      vii. President, Baylor Scott & White Quality Alliance

b. Non-Voting Attendees:
   i. Chief Quality Officer
   ii. Chief Integration Officer
   iii. Chair(s), Patient Safety
   iv. Chair(s), Clinical Effectiveness, Efficiency and Fiscal Impact
   v. Chair(s), Population Health and Equity
   vi. Chair(s), Patient Centeredness/Patient Experience
   vii. Chief Information Officer
   viii. Chief Medical Information Officer
   ix. Chief Medical Information Officer
   x. Senior VP – Legal Counsel and System Risk Officer
   xi. VP for Ancillary Services
   xii. Others as deemed appropriate

4. Oversight Responsibilities / Scope
   a. The Council will have the oversight responsibilities, including, but not limited to:
      i. Review and approve the STEEEP Governance Charter and any changes to the Charters of each subcommittee designated by the Council.
      ii. Review and approve the annual work plans developed by the designated subcommittees identifying STEEEP priorities for BSWH.
      iii. Assure that appropriate resources are provided to support STEEEP priorities.
      iv. Regularly review metrics associated with STEEEP initiatives, as defined and reported by designated subcommittees.
      v. Review and approve a communication plan for communicating the decisions of the Council to BSWH stakeholders.
      vi. Review and approve annual STEEEP care related goals across BSWH, including hospitals, physician groups and clinical service lines.
      vii. Other tasks as designated by the voting members of the Council.
   b. The STEEEP Governance Council is accountable to the BSWH President.

Appendix 16: Physician Leadership Education Needs Assessment

This survey is intended for physician leaders to assess their view of educational topics they would find beneficial to support their leadership activities. It is also intended to assess the optimal time and schedule for this leadership education. The results of this survey will be used to develop a physician leadership curriculum that will be offered in multiple modules over the next year.

PRIORITY EDUCATIONAL NEEDS IN THE AREA OF PHYSICIAN LEADERSHIP (CHECK THE TOP FIVE)

- ☐ Team Building and Leading a Team
- ☐ Project Management and Prioritization
- ☐ Budgets and Financial Statements
- ☐ Dealing with Poor Performance and Disruptive Behavior
- ☐ Transformational Leadership and Leadership Styles
- ☐ Management, Mentoring, and Coaching of Physicians
- ☐ Setting Goals and Measurement of Goals to Achieve Quality and Safety
- ☐ Leading Change
- ☐ Communication Styles and Leadership Effectiveness
- ☐ Negotiation and Conflict Resolution
- ☐ Organizational Strategy
- ☐ Basics of Health Care Information Technology
- ☐ Quality and Process Improvement
- ☐ Patient Safety
- ☐ Emotional Intelligence
- ☐ Health Care Reform and Value-Based Payment
- ☐ Aligning Clinical Initiatives with Organizational Goals

Thank you for your assistance in designing and developing this Physician Leadership Curriculum.

Appendix 17: Physician Leadership Training

INTRODUCTORY PHYSICIAN LEADERSHIP COURSE

Each year, Baylor Scott & White Health (BSWH) senior leaders identify approximately 70 physicians with leadership potential to attend a 1-day leadership course taught by senior physician leaders, a physician from the American College of Physician Executives, and the Greeley Company, an external consulting firm. The program introduces physicians to topics such as "Moving from an Effective Clinician to an Effective Leader," "Medical Staff Management and the Board," "Managing Disruptive Physicians," and "The Importance of Physician Leadership." This course helps physicians behave collaboratively and understand their organizational roles in medical staff leadership and within the health care system (Ballard et al. 2013; Convery, Couch, and Luquire 2012).

ADVANCED PHYSICIAN LEADERSHIP TRAINING

For more experienced physician leaders, BSWH and the Southern Methodist University Cox School of Business offer a course taught in six full-day sessions spread out over 2 years. Fifty physician leaders participate in these courses. The objectives of the Advanced Physician Leadership Training are described in Table A17.1 (Ballard et al. 2013; Convery, Couch, and Luquire 2012).

TABLE A17.1 Key Curriculum Elements in Advanced Physician Leadership Training

Leadership	Analyze their leadership style and develop a plan for improving management effectiveness
	Develop personal awareness and effectiveness in dealing with conflicts and adverse behavior
	Lead effective organizational change initiatives
	Manage through influence, creating more productive and more enjoyable relationships
	Practice the art of leadership
Corporate finance	Use financial information to make better business decisions through health care cost and financial management
	Utilize managerial accounting to improve planning, controlling, and decision making
	Employ financial analysis to better select projects and investments
Strategy	Apply strategic management to compete on the leading edge of turning ideas into business opportunities
	Apply corporate strategy to organizational planning
	Apply human capital strategy in managing performance to evaluate and develop employees

Appendix 18: Nurse Leadership Training

NURSE EXECUTIVE FELLOWSHIP PROGRAM

The Nurse Executive Fellowship program, administered in conjunction with the Southern Methodist University Cox School of Business, prepares Baylor Scott & White Health (BSWH) nurse managers and directors for progressive leadership roles by instilling advanced leadership and business skills. Each year, 25 nurse leaders complete the 1-year fellowship of 12 intensive workshops concluded with significant capstone projects that must have significant impact for the system and a return on investment that a chief financial officer must validate (Ballard et al. 2013).

LEADERSHIP DEVELOPMENT FOR FRONT-LINE NURSES

The ASPIRE (Achieving Synergy in Practice through Impact, Relationships, and Evidence) program is a professional advancement program for front-line nurses. Nurses in the ASPIRE program undertake quality improvement (QI) projects, research studies, and community outreach initiatives to enhance their leadership skills as well as their ability to perform clinical research and practice more effectively (Ballard et al. 2013). Criteria for different ASPIRE leadership levels are presented in Table A18.1.

TABLE A18.1 ASPIRE Leadership Levels

Nursing education	Minimum baccalaureate degree in nursing
Clinical experience	Minimum of 4 years of hospital nursing experience prior to completion of portfolio
National certification	National certification by a recognized professional nursing organization
Learning opportunities/activities	Facilitates/coordinates 2 learning activities; 1 must be outside of unit
Baylor Health Care System (BHCS) professional practice model	Document how you have advocated for your patient or their families during an ethical dilemma and describe how it had an impact on the patient's outcomes
Evidence-based nursing practice	Implement and evaluate an evidence-based practice project (Problem–Intervention–Comparison–Outcome(PICO) question, synthesis table, project description, and results)
Nursing practice	Provide evidence of a project you led to improve outcomes on your unit; include description of activity and pre- and postdata (may reflect evidence-based practice criteria)
Leadership	Provide evidence of how you have engaged others to create a practice change or increase participation in professional activities (shared governance, professional organizations, presentation development, etc.)
Individual learning and professional development	Provide evidence of three learning activities that you have been involved in related to evidence-based practice, quality, leadership, or nursing practice
Best practices	Provide evidence of your participation in an activity or project that has promoted quality or best practices beyond your unit

Appendix 19: STEEEP Academy Leadership Series: Clinical Leadership in Quality Improvement and Patient Safety

The following are the topics for the STEEEP Academy Leadership Series: Clinical Leadership in Quality Improvement and Patient Safety (Figure A19.1).

- The impact of health care reform, value-based purchasing, and other trends on health care delivery
- Leading clinical integration: aligning clinical initiatives with organizational quality and patient safety goals
- Organizing for, mandating, and measuring quality and safety
- Promoting standardized, evidence-based best practices
- Dealing with conflict and fostering teamwork
- Using performance feedback reports to drive changes in clinical practice patterns
- Change management versus managing change
- Steps to achieving sustainable quality and patient safety improvement

FIGURE A19.1 STEEEP Academy Leadership Series: Clinical Leadership in Quality Improvement and Patient Safety.

Appendix 20: Attitudes and Practices of Patient Safety Survey

FIGURE A20.1 Excerpt from Attitudes and Practices of the Patient Safety Survey 2013.

			\<Hospital Name\> Unit Report **Unit Summary (Sorted by Overall Score)**						
Unit Name	**Overall Safety Culture Score**	**Leadership Domain Score**	**Reporting & Feedback Domain Score**	**Resources Domain Score**	**Teamwork Domain Score**	**Physician Partnership Score**	**# of items 5% Above the System % Desirable**	**# of items 5% Below the System % Desirable**
System Score	79.9	75.4	80.5	80.8	82.9	78.4	*na*	*na*
\<Hospital Name\> Score	77.8	73.5	77.8	78.4	81.4	77.3	*na*	*na*
Unit 1	85.0	85.3	83.4	85.6	85.9	86.7	34	0
Unit 2	81.6	80.3	80.6	84.6	81.1	78.7	16	7
Unit 3	81.4	77.4	85.6	79.8	82.8	75.5	19	3
Unit 4	81.2	75.6	79.9	84.2	85.2	82.8	19	5
Unit 5	79.7	76.4	80.8	78.7	83.0	77.8	12	11
Unit 6	79.6	76.3	82.2	78.1	81.9	78.1	15	13
Unit 7	79.5	75.9	82.4	80.1	79.7	77.2	16	7

FIGURE A20.2 Attitudes and Practices of Patient Safety Survey Unit Report.

Appendix 21: Sample Job Descriptions for Community Health Workers

Family: Professional

BAYLOR
Health Care System

JobCode: 402479

Job Description

COMMUNITY HEALTH WORKER I

The Community Health Worker I, is responsible for providing culturally and linguistically appropriate health education, navigation, and/or advocacy services addressing health and social needs.   Successful completion of a Texas Department of State Health Services approved Community Health Worker (CHW) program and related certification is required within six months of hire.

ADDITIONAL REQUIREMENTS:
Certified Medical Assistant preferred
Community Health Worker (CHW): must be able and willing to attend a 160-hour Community Health Worker training course provided through Baylor and obtain CHW certification within six months of employment.
Bilingual English/Spanish strongly preferred

Scope/Impact: -

Job Functions

I. **Assist patients with navigating resources within Baylor Health Care System and within the community.**

   1 Conducts patient assessments, develops patient plans, and conducts and/or navigates patient to appropriate interventions to improve access to care and health status.

   2 Identifies resource options to execute patient plan; assists patients with navigating Baylor Healthcare System and community-based resources supporting health and wellness.

   3 Facilitates communication between patient and his/her providers.

   4 Provides referral and linkage to follow-up services within the community and Baylor Health Care System.

   5 Evaluates achievement of patient plans' objectives.

   6 Develops and maintains knowledge of and relationship with Baylor Health Care System and community-based resources.

II. **Performs basic assessments for patients with chronic disease.**

   1 Obtains basic vital signs, measure height and weight, conduct point of care testing.

   2 Obtains additional basic assessment data, including, but not limited to, literacy, family and social support systems, learning needs and barriers, and knowledge about chronic disease and healthy lifestyle.

Continued...

COMMUNITY HEALTH WORKER I

III. **Following a defined protocol, conducts culturally appropriate, skills building self-management education sessions on different health topics tor groups and individuals.**

   1 Teach basic concepts of health promotion, disease prevention, and self-management.

   2 Provide informal counseling and self-management support.

   3 Apply basic motivational strategies to increase readiness to change and to promote behavior change.

   4 Communicate patient progress with primary care provider.

IV. **Administer evaluation tools to assess program's effectiveness with improvement in health-related activities or linkage to primary or other health care.**

V. **Document plan, goals, and follow-up in a timely manner and communicate to appropriate person.**

VI. **Responsible for tracking work activities and results with close attention to detail.**

VII. **Promote the provision of culturally competent care by educating staff and others within the health care system about beliefs and practices unique and/or relevant to specific populations/groups**

VIII. **Must be able and willing to attend a 160-hour Texas Department of State Health Services Community Health Worker training course provided through Baylor and obtain CHW certification within six months of employment.**

IX. **Maintains Texas Department of State Health Services CHW Certification**

"The essential job functions as stated are intended to describe the general nature and level of work being performed by individuals assigned to this job. The stated job functions are not intended to be construed as an exhaustive list of all job responsibilities, duties and skills required of personnel so classified."

May perform other duties as assigned or requested

License(s)   Certification(s)/Registration(s)

Required Education and/or Experience:

Continued...

COMMUNITY HEALTH WORKER I

Education Required
High School Diploma or GED

Type of Degree

Amount of Experience
1 Plus Years

Type of Experience
Health Care Experience

In Lieu of Education

Amount of Experience

Type of Experience

Organizational Universal Competency Requirements:

Integrity - Models the BHCS values. Establishes trust. Is honest. Demonstrates high ethical and legal standards. Follows regulatory and compliance standards. Is respectful and fair. Holds self and others accountable for demonstrating the values - "Walks the Talk".

Servanthood - Uses power, authority and/or influence constructively. Leads and follows by example. Demonstrates an attitude of unselfish concern. Develops him or herself and supports the development of others. Understands and values the perspective of others.

Quality - Optimizes clinical outcomes. Achieves high quality results. Maintains customer focus. Provides customer value. Provides a safe environment. Continuously improves. Tackles problems head-on and resolves them without delay. Produces good results.

Innovation - Creates and supports new ideas and opportunities that are aligned with BHCS strategic priorities. Leads and adapts to change. Challenges the status quo. Plans appropriately. Solves problems. Exercises sound judgment in solving problems.

Stewardship - Uses resources responsibly. Is accountable. Applies sound judgment. Makes informed decisions. Takes appropriate action. Maintains business and industry knowledge. Works to enhance the fiscal strength of BHCS. Spends time on most important work.

Organizational Core Competency Requirements:

Communication - Communicates openly and in a timely way. Listens to understand. Speaks and writes clearly. Shares information appropriately. Keeps others well informed. Encourages others to share contrary views. Responds in a timely manner to messages/requests.

Adaptability/Flexibility - Deals effectively with change and uncertainty. Copes well with stress and pressure. Is patient. Maintains a positive outlook. Deals constructively with mistakes and setbacks. Looks for ways to help the organization.

Teamwork - Works together to achieve successful outcomes. Seeks input from others. Seeks win-win solutions. Supports a shared purpose. Builds relationships. Supports others to achieve success. Knows when to compromise and find mutually acceptable solutions.

Job Unit Specific Competency:

The immediate supervisor for the unit or work area has the "Unit Specific Position Competencies"

Continued...

COMMUNITY HEALTH WORKER I

	Budgetary Responsibility:		Supervisory Responsibility:
Direct	Budget Amount		Direct
InDirect	Budget Amount		InDirect

Internal Job(s) that would promote to this job:

Internal Job(s) to which this job could promote to:

This Job reports to what Position(s) in the organization:

Potential Safety Hazards:

Family: Professional

BAYLOR
Health Care System

JobCode: 402480

Job Description

COMMUNITY HEALTH WORKER II

The Community Health Worker II is responsible for providing culturally and linguistically appropriate health education, navigation, and/or advocacy services addressing health and social needs.   Successful completion of a Texas Department of State Health Services approved Community Health Worker (CHW) program and related certification is required within six months of hire.

ADDITIONAL REQUIREMENTS:
Certified Medical Assistant preferred
Current Texas Department of State Health Services CHW Certification
Demonstrated CHW competencies (for relevant job functions above)
Bilingual English/Spanish strongly preferre

Scope/Impact: -

Job Functions

I. **Assist patients with navigating resources within Baylor Health Care System and within the community.**

   1 Conducts patient assessments, develops patient plans, and conducts and/or navigates patient to appropriate interventions to improve access to care and health status.

   2 Identifies resource options to execute patient plan; assists patients with navigating Baylor Healthcare System and community-based resources supporting health and wellness.

   3 Facilitates communication between patient and his/her providers.

   4 Provides referral and linkage to follow-up services within the community and Baylor Health Care System.

   5 Evaluates achievement of patient plans' objectives.

   6 Develops and maintains knowledge of and relationship with Baylor Health Care System and community-based resources.

II. **Performs basic assessments for patients with chronic disease.**

   1 Obtains basic vital signs, measure height and weight, conduct point of care testing.

   2 Obtains additional basic assessment data, including, but not limited to, literacy, family and social support systems, learning needs and barriers, and knowledge about chronic disease and healthy lifestyle.

Continued...

COMMUNITY HEALTH WORKER II

III. **Following a defined protocol, conducts culturally appropriate, skills building self-management education sessions on different health topics tor groups and individuals.**

   1 Teach basic concepts of health promotion, disease prevention, and self-management.

   2 Provide informal counseling and self-management support.

   3 Apply basic motivational strategies to increase readiness to change and to promote behavior change.

   4 Communicate patient progress with primary care provider.

IV. **Administer evaluation tools to assess program's effectiveness with improvement in health-related activities or linkage to primary or other health care.**

V. **Document plan, goals, and follow-up in a timely manner and communicate to appropriate person.**

VI. **Responsible for tracking work activities and results with close attention to detail.**

VII. **Promote the provision of culturally competent care by educating staff and others within the health care system about beliefs and practices unique and/or relevant to specific populations/groups**

VIII. **Maintains Texas Department of State Health Services CHW Certification.**

IX. **Mentor/peer trainer for other CHWs, as assigned.**

X. **Coordinates and/or participates in the development of projects related to department as assigned.**

XI. **Participates in departmental committees and quality improvement initiatives as appropriate.**

"The essential job functions as stated are intended to describe the general nature and level of work being performed by individuals assigned to this job. The stated job functions are not intended to be construed as an exhaustive list of all job responsibilities, duties and skills required of personnel so classified."

May perform other duties as assigned or requested

License(s)   Certification(s)/Registration(s)

Required Education and/or Experience:

Continued...

COMMUNITY HEALTH WORKER II

Education Required	**Type of Degree**
High School Diploma or GED	Diploma
Amount of Experience	**Type of Experience**
2 Years of Experience	Health Care Experience

In Lieu of Education

Amount of Experience	**Type of Experience**

Organizational Universal Competency Requirements:

Integrity - Models the BHCS values. Establishes trust. Is honest. Demonstrates high ethical and legal standards. Follows regulatory and compliance standards. Is respectful and fair. Holds self and others accountable for demonstrating the values - "Walks the Talk".

Servanthood - Uses power, authority and/or influence constructively. Leads and follows by example. Demonstrates an attitude of unselfish concern. Develops him or herself and supports the development of others. Understands and values the perspective of others.

Quality - Optimizes clinical outcomes. Achieves high quality results. Maintains customer focus. Provides customer value. Provides a safe environment. Continuously improves. Tackles problems head-on and resolves them without delay. Produces good results.

Innovation - Creates and supports new ideas and opportunities that are aligned with BHCS strategic priorities. Leads and adapts to change. Challenges the status quo. Plans appropriately. Solves problems. Exercises sound judgment in solving problems.

Stewardship - Uses resources responsibly. Is accountable. Applies sound judgment. Makes informed decisions. Takes appropriate action. Maintains business and industry knowledge. Works to enhance the fiscal strength of BHCS. Spends time on most important work.

Organizational Core Competency Requirements:

Communication - Communicates openly and in a timely way. Listens to understand. Speaks and writes clearly. Shares information appropriately. Keeps others well informed. Encourages others to share contrary views. Responds in a timely manner to messages/requests.

Adaptability/Flexibility - Deals effectively with change and uncertainty. Copes well with stress and pressure. Is patient. Maintains a positive outlook. Deals constructively with mistakes and setbacks. Looks for ways to help the organization.

Teamwork - Works together to achieve successful outcomes. Seeks input from others. Seeks win-win solutions. Supports a shared purpose. Builds relationships. Supports others to achieve success. Knows when to compromise and find mutually acceptable solutions.

Job Unit Specific Competency:

The immediate supervisor for the unit or work area has the "Unit Specific Position Competencies"

Continued...

COMMUNITY HEALTH WORKER II

Budgetary Responsibility:		Supervisory Responsibility:
Direct	Budget Amount	Direct
InDirect	Budget Amount	InDirect

Internal Job(s) that would promote to this job:

Internal Job(s) to which this job could promote to:

This Job reports to what Position(s) in the organization:

Potential Safety Hazards:

Appendix 22: STEEEP Care Report: All-Topic All-or-None Care Bundle Compliance

All Topic All-or-None Bundle Compliance
FYTD (July 2013 - June 2014)

Measures	Sys	Fac1	Fac2	Fac3	Fac4	Fac5	Fac6	Fac7	Fac8	Fac9
AON: All or None Bundle (No Comparison Available)	97.3%	95.9% (875/912)	98.6% (137/139)	98.1% (530/540)	95.9% (2,234/2,329)	97.3% (533/548)	97.0% (854/880)	96.2% (535/556)	97.1% (330/340)	99.8% (639/640)
Target: FY14 Target	96.6%	95.8%	98.0%	97.3%	95.0%	97.0%	97.8%	96.0%	96.5%	98.4%
AMI-7a: Fibrinolytic Therapy Received Within 30 Minutes of Hospital Arrival (Benchmark = 100.0%, Threshold = 100.0%)	0.0%	No Cases	No Cases	No Cases	No Cases	0.0%	No Cases	No Cases	No Cases	No Cases
PN-6: Initial Antibiotic Selection for CAP in Immunocompetent Patient (Benchmark = 100.0%, Threshold = 97.0%)	98.4%	97.1%	No Cases	99.3%	96.7%	99.1%	97.2%	98.1%	97.0%	100%
SCIP Card 2: Surgery Patients on Beta-Blocker Therapy Prior to Arrival Who Received a Beta-Blocker During the Perioperative Period (Benchmark = 100.0%, Threshold = 98.0%)	98.7%	96.8%	100%	98.8%	98.8%	99.0%	99.4%	98.2%	98.0%	99.2%
SCIP VTE 2: Surgery Patients Who Received Appropriate Venous Thromboembolism Prophylaxis Within 24 Hours Prior to Surgery To 24 Hours After Surgery (Benchmark = 100.0%, Threshold = 98.0%)	99.5%	99.5%	No Cases	99.5%	99.2%	99.5%	99.8%	98.8%	99.5%	100%
SCIP-Inf-2a: Prophylactic Antibiotic Selection for Surgical Patients (Benchmark = 100.0%, Threshold = 99.0%)	99.5%	99.6%	100%	99.0%	99.6%	97.8%	99.3%	100%	100%	100%
SCIP-Inf-3a: Prophylactic Antibiotics Discontinued Within 24 Hours After Surgery End Time (Benchmark = 100.0%, Threshold = 98.0%)	99.1%	97.9%	100%	99.3%	98.7%	98.4%	98.8%	100%	98.0%	100%

White= at or above the benchmark, Gray= greater than or equal to threshold and below benchmark, Black-bordered box= below threshold.

FIGURE A22.1 All-topic all-or-none bundle compliance scores.

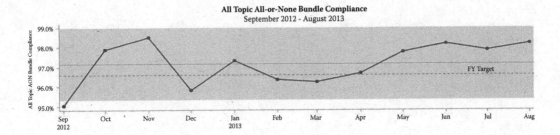

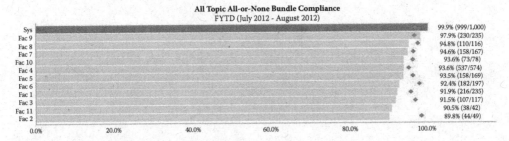

FIGURE A22.2 All-topic all-or-none bundle compliance run chart.

Appendix 23: Diabetes Health and Wellness Institute Model of Diabetes/Chronic Disease Care

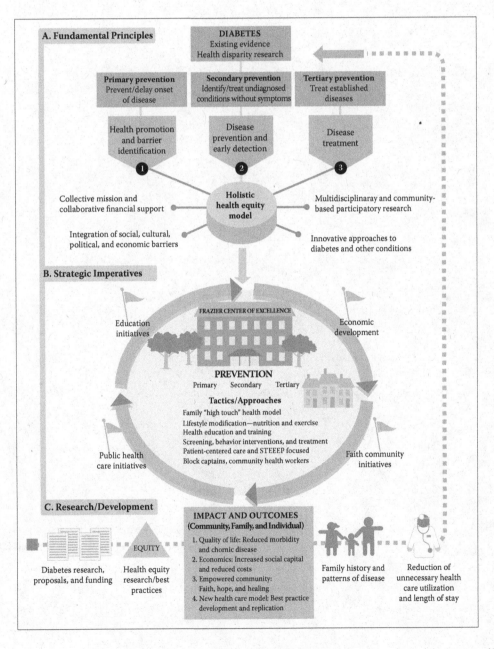

Appendix 24: Sample Learning Boards to Drive Transparency and Employee Engagement

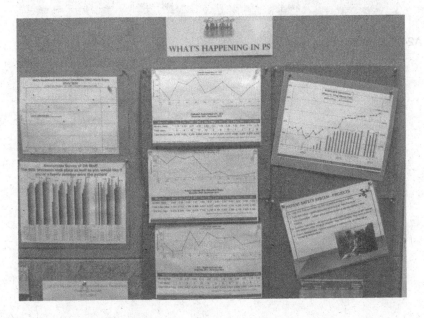

FIGURE A24.1 Sample learning board 1.

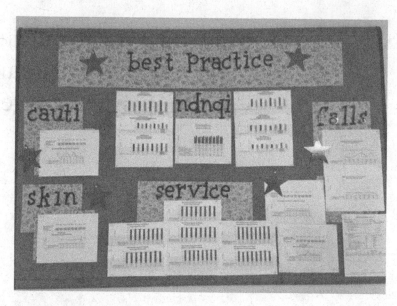

FIGURE A24.2 Sample learning board 2.

Appendix 25: A Quantitative Approach to Goal Setting

In quantitative goal setting, targets are usually determined by modeling using a normal distribution, identifying a "threshold" performance (at which leaders will receive 25% of the portion of their compensation placed at risk); an "intermediate target" performance (corresponding to a 50% award); a "target" performance (at which they receive 100% of the portion of compensation placed at risk); and a "stretch" performance (with this achievement resulting in leaders receiving 150% of the amount of compensation placed at risk). As an example of these performance levels, Table A25.1 shows the fiscal year 2013 performance levels for the Hospital Consumer Assessment of Healthcare Providers and Systems (HCAHPS) Composite Score (one of the service goals).

One challenge associated with goal setting is predicting what performance should be in the future. Performance levels higher and lower than predicted must be defined, and appropriate awards must be associated with each performance level. One way in which prediction can be used to set performance levels is through examining the opportunity for improvement captured in a year. For example, if the average patient satisfaction score improved from the 80th to the 90th percentile in the previous year, then half of the improvement opportunity (the distance between the 80th and 100th percentiles) was captured. In the following year, if half the improvement opportunity again was captured, the average satisfaction score will move from the 90th to the 95th percentile.

Baylor Scott & White Health (BSWH) applies probability rules to its goal setting: The target performance level should have a 50% probability of achievement, and a stretch goal should have a 10% probability. If a performance level has a 90% probability of achievement, it is too easily attainable, and a more challenging goal must be set (Ballard et al. 2013).

TABLE A25.1 Performance Levels for HCAHPS Composite Score for Fiscal Year 2013

Performance Level	HCAHPS Composite Score (Average of the Top Box Averages of All Eight Domains[a])
Threshold	74.8
Intermediate target	75.5
Target	76.1
Stretch	77.3

[a] Communication with doctors, communication with nurses, responsiveness of hospital staff, pain management, communication about medicines, discharge information, cleanliness of the hospital environment, and quietness of the hospital environment.

Appendix 26: Example Reports: Inpatient Mortality and 30-Day Readmission Rates

INPATIENT MORTALITY: SEVERE SEPSIS/SEPTIC SHOCK

About This Report

Metric Development/Reporting: This report was developed to review and track performance for the system and for each facility in key areas of quality and safety. The primary audience is the Board Quality and Safety Committee as well as leaders of all Baylor Scott & White Health (BSWH) facilities.

Development Details

Key system metrics are derived using data from multiple source systems. Metrics are based on definitions developed by the Joint Commission, the Centers for Disease Control and Prevention National Healthcare Safety Network, Centers for Medicare and Medicaid Services, and BSWH (see Figure A26.1).

30-DAY READMISSION RATES

About These Reports

Metric Development/Reporting: These reports were developed to review the percentages of readmissions for two patient age groups, 18+ and 65+, patients with a primary diagnosis of acute myocardial infarction, chronic obstructive pulmonary disease, heart failure, pneumonia, and total hip/total knee arthroplasty. These reports help stakeholders track the effects of interventions (Figure A26.2).

Development Details

Administrative data are used to develop reports and associated patient lists. Calculations include a 3-month rolling percentage, which is the product of readmission cases divided by index cases. The measure definition is based on what has been published by the Centers for Medicare and Medicaid Services.

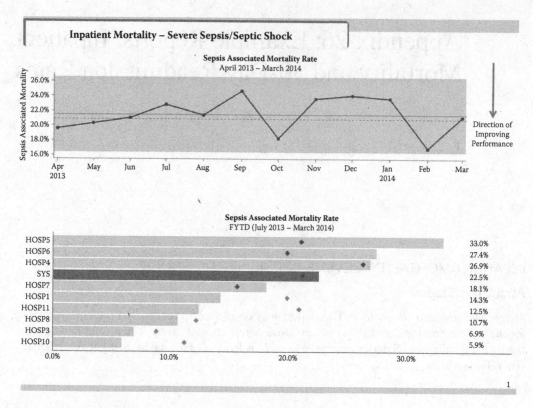

FIGURE A26.1 Inpatient mortality: severe sepsis and septic shock.

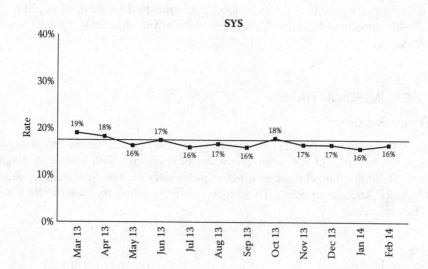

FIGURE A26.2 Heart failure 30-day all-cause readmission rate.

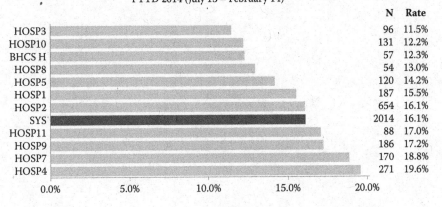

BHCS HF 30 – Day All Cause Readmission Rate
FYTD 2014 (July 13 – February 14)

	N	Rate
HOSP3	96	11.5%
HOSP10	131	12.2%
BHCS H	57	12.3%
HOSP8	54	13.0%
HOSP5	120	14.2%
HOSP1	187	15.5%
HOSP2	654	16.1%
SYS	2014	16.1%
HOSP11	88	17.0%
HOSP9	186	17.2%
HOSP7	170	18.8%
HOSP4	271	19.6%

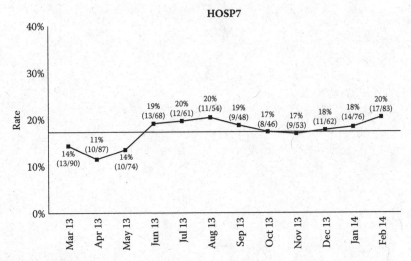

FIGURE A26.2 (*Continued*)

Appendix 27: Areas of Focus for Key Department of Patient Safety Personnel

Job Title	Key Areas of Focus
Director of patient safety	• Serve as an expert resource throughout the organization for identifying and creating a body of knowledge related to patient safety • Provide leadership and guidance in the further development and dissemination of patient safety information, including data designed to promote knowledge transfer, best practices, information sharing, and innovative problem solving
Manager of patient safety	• Monitor patient safety data for trends and recommend changes as appropriate to improve the safety of care throughout the organization • Provide strategic, operational, and analytic leadership related to patient safety
Patient safety measurement specialist	• Manage Department of Patient Safety coordination of National Patient Safety Goals, adverse event measurement tool, and other patient safety initiatives via surveys, audits for interrater reliability checks, end-user validation, data extraction, and other related activities • Develop and maintain a high level of expertise in patient safety • Assist clinician leaders in monitoring processes shown to be effective in improving patient safety
Human factors engineer	• Assist in the analysis of facility needs to include workflow analysis, space programming and functional layout design; may apply simulation technology to this process • Utilize a systems approach to conduct operational analyses of organizational or departmental systems and processes, applying various industrial engineering techniques; work closely with department management or teams throughout the process and during implementation of recommendations • Participate in quality improvement (QI) teams and provide technical support to assist the teams with use of QI tools and the collection and analysis of data; may also serve as team leader or facilitator of a QI team

Appendix 28: Areas of Focus for Key Department of Patient Experience Personnel

Job Title	Key Areas of Focus
Director of patient experience	• Oversee the strategies and activities of patient satisfaction survey processes across the organization to provide regular data and trends to enable quality improvement (QI) to serve internal customers • Facilitate the strategies and activities of organizational physician satisfaction survey processes, working with executives and medical staff leaders on action plans and outcomes of these plans • Ensures the patient satisfaction data used to meet Centers for Medicare and Medicaid Services (CMS) criteria for reporting and reimbursement purposes follow CMS regulations
Manager of patient experience	• Lead a team of coaches and facilitate an organizational council to support program objectives and patient satisfaction results • Assess, design, deploy, and interpret performance metrics related to customer loyalty, operational excellence, and compliance assessment
Education manager	• Lead the strategic alignment, assessment, identification, development or selection, implementation, and measurement of education and learning methods, programs, and processes that enhance individual and organizational effectiveness • Select, develop, and orient new and entry-level trainers and internal faculty to processes, facilitation methods, and course materials to enhance individual effectiveness • Facilitate system educational and learning programs
Quality improvement consultant	• Act as a resource to organizational teams and various projects and serve as a trusted change agent related to various groups and individuals charged with clinical and nonclinical QI • Track budgetary implications of QI projects and work with finance/decision support to identify not only the costs associated with implementation of QI initiatives but also the clinical and financial returns on investment • Coordinate and review both organizational and facility data and processes to develop and execute plans to resolve any QI issues
Outcomes data analyst	• Use available databases to analyze and benchmark criteria against organizational facilities and other facilities to assist in QI activities • Coordinate activities related to Texas Health Care Information Collection

Appendix 29: Eight Fundamental Service Behaviors

AIDET (registered trademark of the Studer Group) stands for Acknowledge, Introduce, Duration, Explanation, and Thank You. In a clinical setting, this formula for communicating reduces fear and anxiety. AIDET is useful in any setting to introduce yourself and set expectations.

Bedside Shift Report is a handoff report between caregivers and the patient/family during a shift change. Handoff reports are valuable on any project that involves multiple people or teams.

Care Calls are opportunities to check on a patient and make sure the patient is okay and has the help needed within 24–48 hours of the patient's discharge from the facility.

Hourly Rounding is a standardized process of assessing a patient's needs and addressing concerns in a proactive manner. All of us "round"—or we should. We check with our coworkers and others who rely on us to make sure we are meeting their needs in our work environment.

Leader Rounding for Outcomes is a unit leader-focused interview with patients and families that ensures the unit culture supports patient-centered outcomes.

Managing Up refers to talking to patients about each member of the team in a positive light, which creates team alignment, not division. This is a behavior that everyone should practice and can be used across the system.

Narration of Care means communicating so that patients understand their goals for the day; the plan of care for their stay; the purpose of tests, treatments, medication with side effects, relevant results and impact; and progress toward discharge. In a business setting, you practice this behavior when you give status reports or presentations.

Open Access is a health care environment that encourages and fosters inclusion of a family member, friend, or other individual, known as the Primary Support Person, for emotional support for the patient 24 hours a day.

Appendix 30: Blood Utilization Dashboard

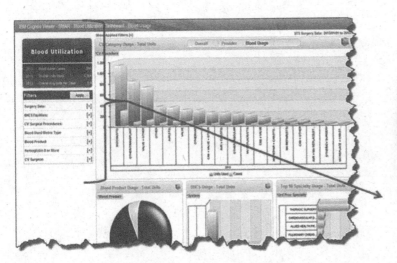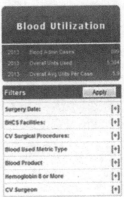

FIGURE A30.1 Sample blood utilization dashboard.

Appendix 31: Baylor Scott & White Quality Alliance Data Architecture and Example Screen Shots from the Baylor Scott & White Quality Alliance Dashboard

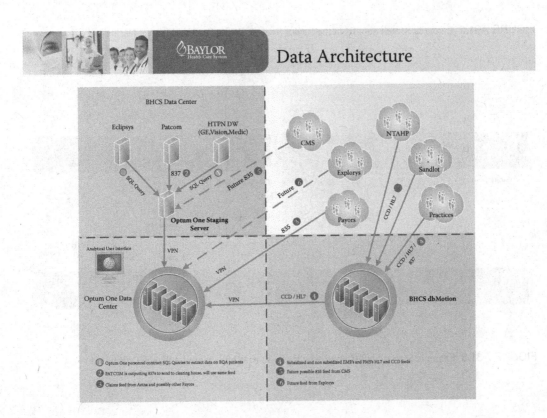

FIGURE A31.1 Baylor Scott & White Quality Alliance Data Architecture

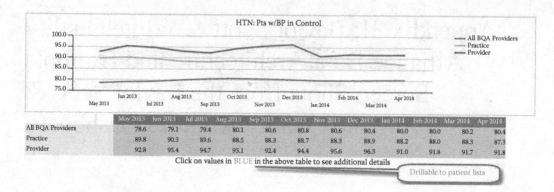

FIGURE A31.2 Example Screen Shot from the Baylor Scott & White Quality Alliance Dashboard

	May 2013	Jun 2013	Jul 2013	Aug 2013	Sep 2013	Oct 2013	Nov 2013	Dec 2013	Jan 2014	Feb 2014	Mar 2014	Apr 2014
All BQA Providers	78.6	79.1	79.4	80.1	80.6	80.8	80.6	80.4	80.0	80.0	80.2	80.4
Practice	89.8	90.3	89.6	88.5	88.3	88.7	88.3	88.9	88.2	88.0	88.3	87.3
Provider	92.8	95.4	94.7	93.1	92.4	94.4	95.6	96.3	91.0	91.8	91.7	91.8

Click on values in BLUE in the above table to see additional details

Drillable to patient lists

Clinical Integration

Metric Name	Current Period	Prior Period	Target	Percentile Ranking
View BQA Website Goal: 8 out of 12 months	143% 10 of 7 YTD	100% 12 of 12	66.7%	98th Percentile

Quality

Metric Name	Current Period	Prior Period	Target	Percentile Ranking
Adult Preventive Services Audit (Practice Totals Only)	Provider Results Coming Soon			
Diabetes Audit (Practice Totals Only)	Provider Results Coming Soon			
HTN: Pts w/BP in Control	91.8% 05/01/2013 to 04/30/2014	91.7% 04/30/2013 to 03/31/2014		97th Percentile

Service

Metric Name	Current Period	Prior Period	Target	Percentile Ranking

Utilization Efficiency

Metric Name	Current Period	Prior Period	Target	Percentile Ranking
Generic Prescribing Rate	80.4% YTD through: 06/29/2014	68.5% 1/1/2013 to 12/31/2013		

FIGURE A31.3 Example Screen Shot from the Baylor Scott & White Quality Alliance Dashboard

Appendix 32: Sample Performance Award Program Measurements

FY14 PAP Approved System & Facility Measurements

Area of Focus	Metric	Goal level	Hospital A	Hospital B	Hospital C	Hospital D	Hospital E	Hospital F	Hospital G	Hospital H	Hospital I	Hospital J	Hospital K	Hospital L
People	1st Yr. Voluntary Retension													
		threshold	87.3%											
		intermed target	88.0%		System		System							
		target	88.7%											
		maximum	90.8%											
	All Employee Voluntary Retention													
		threshold	89.3%											
		intermed target	89.4%		System		System							
		target	90.2%											
		maximum	91.6%											
Quality	All or None Core Measures													
		threshold	96.3%	95.2%		97.3%			96.6%	97.2%		95.6%	96.2%	
		intermed target	96.4%	95.4%	System	97.5%	System	SD	96.9%	97.4%	SD	95.7%	96.3%	SD
		target	96.6%	95.8%		98.0%			97.5%	97.8%		96.0%	96.5%	
		maximum	96.8%	96.1%		98.2%			97.7%	98.0%		96.3%	96.8%	
	Inpatient Mortality Reduction													
		threshold	0.7%	0.4%					0.8%	0.7%		0.6%	0.6%	
		intermed target	1.4%	0.8%	System	N/A	System	N/A	1.7%	1.4%	N/A	1.2%	1.2%	N/A
		target	3.0%	1.5%					3.5%	2.8%		2.5%	2.5%	
		maximum	4.4%	2.3%					5.1%	4.2%		3.8%	3.8%	
	30 Day Readmission for AMI, HF and PN													
		threshold	15.0%	17.5%		7.6%			18.5%	13.3%		14.5%	15.0%	
		intermed target	14.8%	17.3%	System	7.4%	System	N/A	18.3%	13.1%	N/A	14.3%	14.8%	N/A
		target	14.5%	17.0%		7.1%			18.0%	12.8%		14.0%	14.5%	
		maximum	14.0%	16.5%		6.6%			17.5%	12.3%		13.5%	14.0%	
	Asthma													
		threshold									32.5%			
		intermed target	N/A	N/A	N/A	N/A	N/A	N/A	N/A	N/A	33.3%	N/A	N/A	N/A
		target									35.0%			
		maximum									36.5%			
	Diabetes BP													
		threshold									64.6%			
		intermed target	N/A	N/A	N/A	N/A	N/A	N/A	N/A	N/A	64.8%	N/A	N/A	N/A
		target									64.9%			
		maximum									65.4%			
Service	Emergency Dept (mean score)													

FIGURE A32.1 Performance award program (PAP)-approved system and facility measurements.

Appendix 33: Sample Safe Surgery Saves Lives Checklist[*]

SIGN IN (BEFORE INDUCTION OF ANESTHESIA)

☐ Patient/designee has confirmed: identity, site, procedure, consent
☐ Site marked/not applicable
   ☐ Anesthesia safety check completed
   ☐ Anesthesia TIME OUT
Known allergy?
☐ Yes ☐ No
Difficult airway/aspiration risk?
☐ No ☐ Yes, and equipment/assistance available
Type and crossmatch done?
☐ Yes ☐ No
☐ Need for beta-blockers addressed

TIME OUT/PAUSE (BEFORE SKIN INCISION)

☐ Confirm all team members have been introduced by name and role and actively participate
   Briefing:
☐ Positioning
☐ Implants/special equipment/supplies
☐ Instrumentation
☐ Sterility (including indicator results) has been confirmed?
☐ TIME OUT: Surgical team verbally confirms correct patient, procedure, position, side and site; surgical site marking visible after patient prepped and draped; accurate consent form:
   at _____ (time)
☐ TIME OUT: for new physician or new procedure:
   at _____ (time)
☐ Surgeon reviews: Critical or unexpected steps; operative duration, anticipated blood loss—risk of greater than 500 mL blood loss (7 mL/kg in children); need to administer antibiotics or fluids for irrigation

---

[*] World Health Organization. Safe Surgery. http://www.who.int/patientsafety/safesurgery/en. Accessed July 25, 2014.

Antibiotic prophylaxis given within the last 60 minutes? (120 minutes for vancomycin and fluoroquinilones)

☐ Yes _____ IV (medication) at _____ (time)
☐ Not applicable

Is essential imaging properly labeled and displayed?

☐ Yes ☐ Not applicable

SIGN OUT (BEFORE PATIENT LEAVES OPERATING ROOM)

RN verbally confirms with the team:

☐ The name of the procedure completed and wound classification
☐ Instrument, sponge, and needle counts are completed (or not applicable)
☐ All specimens appropriately labeled and sent (including patient name)
☐ Whether there are any equipment or other problems to be addressed
☐ Surgical team reviews the key concerns for recovery and management of this patient

RN Signature: _____ Date: _____ Time:_____

Appendix 34: Cardiovascular Surgery Quality Council Charter

PURPOSE

The purpose of the Cardiovascular Surgery Quality Council is to provide a formal organizational structure and oversight for activities and initiatives related to cardiovascular and thoracic surgery along the entire continuum of care. This will minimize redundancies in cardiovascular and thoracic surgery quality efforts, resulting in a model that is evidence based, cohesive, and comprehensive. Through encouragement of collaboration between areas of care that involve cardiovascular and cardiothoracic surgery for all of our patient populations, the council will serve as a sounding board and gatekeeper for current and future quality-related endeavors. This will ensure that actions taken by individuals across the system are aligned with the fiduciary and strategic responsibilities of leadership and the overall mission of the organization. The council will be granted the power and authority to set system-wide policies, rules, and procedures. The initial work of the council was performed by the Cardiovascular Surgery Best Care Group.

GOALS

- Provide oversight for quality improvement (QI) activities for the cardiovascular and cardiothoracic surgery service line
- Provide a structure with authority to perform organizational quality reviews related to patient-specific process and outcomes
- Recommend system-wide policies and procedures for the cardiovascular and cardiothoracic surgery service line
- Recommend, initiate, and oversee system-wide QI efforts for the cardiovascular and cardiothoracic service line

BACKGROUND

In 2007, a group of cardiothoracic surgeons, nurses, administrators, and other stakeholders began meeting to review data, identify areas of improvement, and discuss facility-level QI opportunities. This group has met every 6 months since 2007, and most recently, the surgeon component of this group began reviewing and discussing cardiac surgeon process and outcomes data. Baylor Health Care System (BHCS) was the first health care system in North Texas to begin this type of activity, and its model has been adopted by other regional health care systems.

Since 2007, the attendance, collegiality, satisfaction, and effectiveness of the group attending these meetings have increased substantially, resulting in a June 2012 request by the group for an integrated, system-wide, and formally sanctioned structure to manage cardiothoracic surgery QI efforts.

MEMBERSHIP

Members were selected to represent various points along the continuum of care. Additional individuals may be called on to attend meetings on an ad hoc basis depending on the subject matter. Initial membership (both surgeon and nonsurgeon) was approved during the initial formation of the council. Surgeons were appointed for 2-year periods, with renewals or replacements on resignation subject to approval by the organization's medical director of cardiovascular surgery, chief medical officer, and chief quality officer or associate chief quality officer.

This council reports to

- The organization's chief quality officer and chief medical officer
- The appropriate individual hospital quality councils in its quality review role
- The president or leader of the organization's cardiovascular service line in its operational and strategic roles

Appendix 35: Case Studies: Driving STEEEP Care through Quality Improvement

CASE STUDY: DECREASING VENTILATOR MORTALITY IN THE INTENSIVE CARE UNIT

Background

Evidence-based research shows that early mobility in patients with respiratory failure is safe and beneficial for those critically ill. In May 2011, nurses attending a national critical care conference learned new evidence-based practices related to early mobility while on the ventilator. The nurses were eager to put this new knowledge into clinical practice. A multidisciplinary team developed or revised practices and protocols to increase mobility and facilitate earlier withdrawal of ventilator support by:

- Increasing multidisciplinary rounding to daily from three times a week
- Revising the ventilator checklist to include a new mobility protocol
- Increasing spontaneous breathing trials (SBTs) to twice daily

Aim Statement

By December 31, 2012, the hospital intensive care unit (ICU) aimed to decrease its Hospital-Standardized Mortality Ratio–Texas (HSMR-TX) for patients on ventilators to a ratio of less than one (1) per quarter. This was done through an effort to decrease ventilator days of non-chronic ventilator-dependent patients to less than 2.5 days per patient per week by

1. Performing daily multidisciplinary goal-directed rounds
2. Performing spontaneous breathing trials twice daily
3. Initiating an early progressive mobility protocol
4. Revising the ventilator checklist to include these goals and monitoring its use

Interventions

Interventions are presented in Figure A35.1.

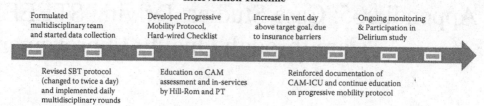

FIGURE A35.1 Intervention timeline.

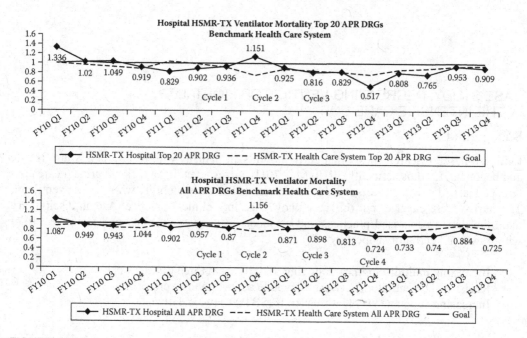

FIGURE A35.2 Hospital-standardized mortality ratios.

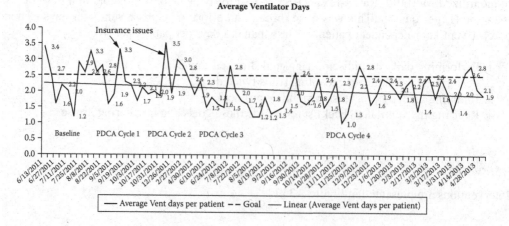

FIGURE A35.3 Average ventilator days.

Results

The HSMR remains under the goal and under the hospital system benchmark. Ventilator days (time on ventilator) average below the goal of 2.5 days per week (see Figures A 35.2 and A 35.3).

Conclusion

Because of the project's success in improving care, the facility began using the mobility protocol and practices for all ICU patients, not just those on the ventilator. Several aspects of this project have become part of the system's ventilator order sets. The project was chosen as one of the top three for the Innovations Award at the Texas Hospital Association Annual Meeting in February 2013 in Austin, Texas, where a presentation was made for the Innovations session. In addition, a poster was presented at the Texas Association for Healthcare Quality meeting in Austin in October 2012. It received first place in poster judging and many positive comments. The project has led to multiple in-services for improved care of ventilator patients at local long-term care facilities.

CASE STUDY: PROJECT RE-ENGINEERING DISCHARGE (RED)

Background

Nearly 20% of Medicare hospitalizations are followed by readmission within 30 days, and approximately 90% of these rehospitalizations within 30 days are unplanned, the result of clinical deterioration. Only 50% of patients rehospitalized within 30 days had a physician visit before readmission. In addition, 19% of Medicare discharges are followed by an adverse event within 30 days, and 66% of these events are adverse drug events, the kind most often judged to be preventable. Project Re-Engineering Discharge (RED) is a research group at Boston University Medical Center that develops and tests strategies to improve the hospital discharge process in a way that promotes patient safety and reduces readmissions. A facility participated in the Texas Hospital Association Project RED collaborative sponsored through an Agency for Healthcare Research and Quality (AHRQ) grant.

Aim Statement

Implementation of Project RED strategies at a facility was to result in a cumulative all-cause composite readmission rate of less than 11.5% for acute myocardial infarction (AMI), pneumonia (PN), and heart failure (HF) patients discharged to home from the fourth and fifth floor.

Interventions

- Made a clear and decisive statement
- Identified implementation leadership
- Analyzed readmission rates and determined goal
- Identified which patients should receive the RED
- Created process map
- Revised current discharge workflow to eliminate duplication
- Assigned responsibility for RED components
- Trained discharge educators and follow-up telephone callers
- Decided how to generate the "After Hospital Care Plan"
- Provided the RED strategies for diverse populations
- Planned to measure the progress of RED implementation

Results

The composite all-cause 30-day readmission rate for the target Project RED population (acute myocardial infarction, pneumonia, and heart failure patients discharged to home from the fourth and fifth floor) surpassed the goal of less than 11.5% (see Figure A35.4).

- Initial rate: 18.8% (December 2011)
- Cumulative rate: 10.4% (May 2012)
- Represents a 44.7% decrease during the 6-month period

Conclusion

Implementation of Project RED strategies reduced unplanned 30-day readmissions among patients with acute myocardial infarction, pneumonia, and heart failure.

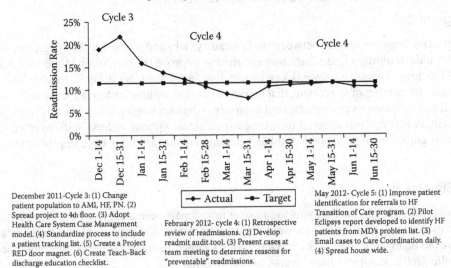

30 Day Cumulative Readmission Rate
Target: Hospital Readmission Rate Goal ≤ 11.5%

December 2011-Cycle 3: (1) Change patient population to AMI, HF, PN. (2) Spread project to 4th floor. (3) Adopt Health Care System Case Management model. (4) Standardize process to include a patient tracking list. (5) Create a Project RED door magnet. (6) Create Teach-Back discharge education checklist.

February 2012- cycle 4: (1) Retrospective review of readmissions. (2) Develop readmit audit tool. (3) Present cases at team meeting to determine reasons for "preventable" readmissions.

May 2012- Cycle 5: (1) Improve patient identification for referrals to HF Transition of Care program. (2) Pilot Eclipsys report developed to identify HF patients from MD's problem list. (3) Email cases to Care Coordination daily. (4) Spread house wide.

FIGURE A35.4 Composite all-cause 30-day readmission rate.

CASE STUDY: IMPROVING LABORATORY AND EMERGENCY DEPARTMENT SPECIMEN TURNAROUND TIMES

Background

In an effort to improve service between the laboratory (lab) and the emergency department (ED) staff, a multidisciplinary Lean team was assigned to improve the turnaround time for lab specimens. The team uncovered several key factors that influenced the delay of results. The main factor was the number of specimens that arrived in the lab without orders. Process failures were studied, and solutions were implemented to ensure orders accompanied specimens from the ED to the lab. A process was created to manage specimens without orders. Staff were educated, collection guides were developed, and blue specimen biohazard bags were implemented.

Aim Statement

By March 31, 2012, the facility was to improve intradepartmental service between the ED and the lab by ensuring that specimens were obtained correctly and processed in a timely manner. This was to be evidenced by a 5% reduction in specimen turnaround times for comprehensive metabolic profile, complete blood count, and urinalysis.

Interventions

- Processed changes in both the ED and lab to ensure orders are entered before the specimen leaves the ED
- Improved recognition and prioritization of ED specimens by development of visual cues
- Educated of ED and lab staff related to correct tube and quantity of blood required for each test

Results

The results are shown in Figure A35.5.

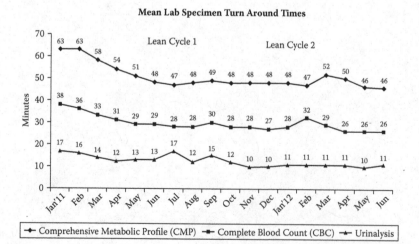

FIGURE A35.5 Mean laboratory specimen turnaround times.

Conclusion

After the interventions were implemented, a decrease in turnaround time (in minutes) was observed for comprehensive metabolic profile (from 63 to 46 or 27%); complete blood count (from 38 to 26 or 32%); and urinalysis (from 17 to 11 or 35%). These results suggest that changes such as staff education, development of visual cues, and order entry process improvements can decrease turnaround specimen times and improve service between ED and lab staff.

CASE STUDY: ACT III ELECTRONIC HEALTH RECORD PROVIDER TRAINING

Background

Government mandates (American Recovery and Reinvestment Act) require eligible hospitals to adopt and demonstrate meaningful use of electronic health record (EHR) technology by 2015 to avoid reduction in Medicare reimbursements. As a hospital (facility D) transitioned 1,542 medical staff and allied health and house staff from voluntary electronic documentation to the physician order management phase of the EHR, the goal was to provide every possible opportunity for education prior to implementation. Key stakeholders from the medical staff, administration, and other user groups were identified to develop an effective education plan. Failing to educate providers in a timely manner or educating them too soon jeopardizes patient safety, quality of care, and working relationships.

Aim Statement

By February 2, 2013, 85% of high-activity providers and house staff (i.e., tier 1, 809 totals) were to be educated in Act III EHR Computerized Physician Order Management (CPOM). This was to be accomplished, beginning in November 2012, by facilitating communication and follow-up with providers through medical staff department chiefs, administration, and communicators.

Interventions

- A communicator was moved to the Medical Staff Services office.
- Medical Staff Service personnel assisted with scheduling appointments.
- Daily reports were sent to administration, education, informatics, chiefs, and division heads.
- A communicator was added to divide responsibilities for follow-up and scheduling.
- Availability of education time slots was increased.
- Certified letters were sent to noncompliant providers.
- Physician one-on-one appointments and ongoing superuser support for efficient workflow were established.

See Figures A 35.6 and 35.7 for more information.

Results

As of March 2013, of Tier 1 providers, 99% were trained.

Conclusion

Information on the providers trained across facilities is presented in Figure A35.7.

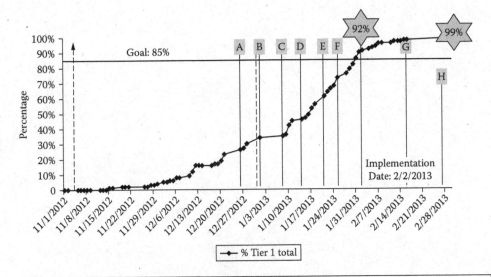

A– Communicator moved to Medical Staff Services office
B – Medical Staff Service personnel assisted with scheduling appointments
C – Started sending daily reports sent to administration, education, informatics, chiefs, and division heads
D – Additional communicator added to divide responsibilities for follow-up and scheduling
E – Increased availability of education time slots
F – Certified letters sent to non-compliant providers
G – Physician one-on-one appointments and ongoing super user support for efficient workflow
H – As of March 2013, 99% Tier 1 providers trained

FIGURE A35.6 Percentage of tier 1 providers trained.

Implemen-tation Date	Facility	Total Providers (July '13)	Total Providers Educated	% Providers Educated	Total Tier 1 Providers	Total Tier 1 Educated	% Tier 1 Educated
Feb 2012	A	829	308	37%	71	48	68%
July 2012	B	584	444	76%	N/A	N/A	N/A
Aug 2012	C	479	Data Unavailable	Data Unavailable	122	99	81%
Feb 2013	D	1,542	1,311	85%	809	745	92%
Apr 2013	E	999	409	41%	149	134	90%
Jun 2013	F	520	260	50%	201	180	90%

FIGURE A35.7 Providers trained across facilities.

Appendix 36: Trauma Readmission Analysis

Trauma Readmission Analysis (DML)

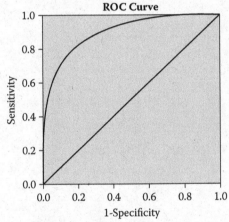

ROC Curve

Diagonal segments are produced by ties

FIGURE A36.1 Trauma readmission analysis.

Area Under the Curve

Test Result Variable(s): PRE_1 Predicted probability

Area	Std. Error[a]	Asymptotic Sig.[b]	Asymptotic 95% Confidence Interval	
			Lower Bound	Upper Bound
0.901	0.006	0.00	0.888	0.913

The test result variable(s): PRE_1 Predicted probability has at least one tie between the positive actual state group and the negative actual state group. Statistics may be biased.

a. Under the nonparametric assumption

b. Null hypothesis: true area = 0.5

Bibliography

Ballard, D.J. 2003. Indicators to improve clinical quality across an integrated health care system. *International Journal for Quality in Health Care* 15 (Suppl 1): i13–23.

Ballard, D.J., N.S. Fleming, J.T. Allison, P.B. Convery, and R. Luquire, eds. 2013. *Achieving STEEEP Health Care*. Boca Raton, FL: CRC Press.

Ballard, D.J., B. Spreadbury, and R.S. Hopkins 3rd. 2004. Health care quality improvement across the Baylor Health Care System: The first century. *Proceedings* (Baylor University Medical Center) 17 (3): 277–288.

Berwick, D.M., T.W. Nolan, and J. Whittington. 2008. The triple aim: Care, health, and cost. *Health Affairs* (Millwood) 27 (3): 759–769.

Casanova, J. 2008. Medical staffs and nursing staffs: The need for joint leadership. *Physician Executive Journal* 34 (6): 24–27.

Centers for Medicare and Medicaid Services. 2014. EHR Incentive Programs. https://www.cms.gov/Regulations-and-Guidance/Legislation/EHRIncentivePrograms/index.html?redirect=/ehrincentiveprograms (accessed May 3, 2014).

Convery, P., C.E. Couch, and R. Luquire. 2012. Training physician and nursing leaders for performance improvement. In *From Front Office to Front Line: Essential Issues for Health Care Leaders*, ed. S. Berman, pp. 59–85. Oakbrook Terrace, IL: The Joint Commission.

Corrigan, J.M., M.S. Donaldson, L.T. Kohn, S.K. Maguire, and K.C. Pike. 2001. *Crossing the Quality Chasm: A New Health System for the 21st Century*. Washington, DC: National Academy Press.

Haynes, A.B., T.G. Weiser, W.R. Berry, S.R. Lipsitz, A.H. Breizat, E.P. Dellinger, T. Herbosa, et al. 2009. A surgical safety checklist to reduce morbidity and mortality in a global population. *New England Journal of Medicine* 360 (5): 491–499.

Herrin, J., D. Nicewander, and D.J. Ballard. 2008. The effect of health care system administrator pay-for-performance on quality of care. *The Joint Commission Journal on Quality and Patient Safety* 34 (11): 646–654.

Joint Commission. n.d. Core Measure Sets. http://www.jointcommission.org/core_measure_sets.aspx (accessed April 22, 2014).

Kennerly, D., K.M. Richter, V. Good, J. Compton, and D.J. Ballard. 2011. Journey to no preventable risk: The Baylor Health Care System patient safety experience. *American Journal of Medical Quality* 26 (1): 43–52.

Kennerly, D.A., M. Saldaña, R. Kudyakov, B. da Graca, D. Nicewander, and J. Compton. 2013. Description and evaluation of adaptations to the Global Trigger Tool to enhance value to adverse event reduction efforts. *Journal of Patient Safety* 9 (2): 87–95.

Loshin, D. 2010, June. *Operationalizing Data Governance through Data Policy Management*. Knowledge Integrity.

Medicare.gov. n.d. Hospital Compare. https://data.medicare.gov/data/hospital-compare (accessed April 22, 2014).

Patient Protection and Affordable Care Act. Public Law 111–148, March 23, 2010. 124 Stat. 119. http://www.gpo.gov/fdsys/pkg/PLAW-111publ148/pdf/PLAW-111publ148.pdf.

Raths, D. Bringing Physicians out of a "Data-Poor Environment." *Healthcare Informatics*. May 16, 2013.

Stoller, J.K. 2009. Developing physician-leaders: A call to action. *Journal of General Internal Medicine* 24 (7): 876–878.

World Health Organization. Safe Surgery. http://www.who.int/patientsafety/safesurgery/en. Accessed July 25, 2014.

Index

Printed in the United States
by Baker & Taylor Publisher Services

Printed in the United States
by Baker & Taylor Publisher Services